The Hip, High-Prote, Low-Cal, Easy-Does-It Cookbook

The Hip, High-Prote, Low-Cal, Easy-Does-It Cookbook

BY NAURA HAYDEN

Dodd, Mead & Company · New York

ISBN: 0-396-06516-3
Library of Congress Catalog Card Number: 78-39224
Printed in the United States of America
by The Haddon Craftsmen, Inc., Scranton, Penna.

TO LOVE, WHICH IS GOD

To Begin With

THIS BOOK is for lifeguards, doormen, animal trainers, nurses, racing drivers, florists, policemen, models, conductors (symphony and streetcar), shoemakers, salesgirls, fishmongers, window washers, neurotics (in any field), stewardesses, kids, lawyers, authors, dress manufacturers, brain surgeons, movie stars, engineers (civil and railroad), hairdressers, pharmacists, lighthouse keepers—EVERYBODY IN THE WHOLE WORLD—because every human being needs complete protein every single day to be truly healthy. Many people get fewer than 25 grams a day and don't even know that they need a minimum of 70 grams a day for cell growth and renewal. No wonder muscles are saggy, colds are frequent, teeth are cavitied, skin is wrinkly, and nerves are bad. But it's never too late. You can now discover which foods contain complete protein and which do not. Here are nearly two hundred delicious recipes for super-high-protein dishes, with a count of all the complete protein in each one.

So to stay in top shape, don't count calories—count protein grams! Read on and you'll understand why and how. You'll see that if you start filling yourself with prote instead of just cals, you'll look and feel better and have more *real* energy than you've ever had in your whole life!

Contents

Introduction

THEY LAUGHED WHEN I disappeared into the kitchen, and I didn't even say anything funny. I guess they didn't expect me, an actress, to be able to boil water right—but I fooled 'em.

Cooking was always the only household chore I liked. I hated dusting and vacuuming and all that jazz. But cooking was different. It was fun. I felt completely free in the kitchen—free to create and concoct any wild dish I could imagine. And I came up with some pretty terrific recipes.

Psychologists say that love and food are very closely tied together, that when you give food you're giving love. That's why cooking is fun, because it's an act of love. What more loving thing can we do for ourselves and others than to produce delicious food that pleasures the palate and truly nourishes the body?

As a kid I had a ball with cakes and pies and cookies and candies. I was the Renoir of the kitchen, whipping up whatever turned me on. It wasn't until I was a late teen-ager that I got into nutrition. Not that I wanted to learn about it. I was forced into it. At the tender age of nineteen I started to fall apart, and even before that all kinds of things were going wrong. A touch on the arm produced bruises. My gums would bleed whenever I brushed my teeth. Canker sores—tiny ulcers of the mouth—were so painful I could hardly talk, and from early childhood I got them frequently. Everything seemed to be wrong. Then finally I found myself in Cedars of Lebanon Hospital in Los Angeles, horizontal for weeks on end with some elusive malady none of the learned doctors could diagnose. I felt awful.

At this low point in my life, a friend brought me a copy of Adelle Davis's *Let's Eat Right to Keep Fit.* SHAZAM—instant revelation! "Bruises and bleeding gums are both important danger signals," I read. "When adequate Vitamin C is added to the diet, however, the capillary walls become strong within 24 hours." So I tried it, and to this day there's nary a bruise on me, and my gums stopped bleeding. Fantastic! Canker sores, the book said, were a result of tension and could be cured by a daily dose of powdered brewer's yeast. Fifteen minutes after my first glass the sores disappeared—honest. Again, a star for Adelle. (Later I learned the problem came from all the sugar and candy I consumed, which use up the B vitamins and leave one pretty nervous.)

Although there are some hip, open-minded, nutrition-wise doctors, many study for years to learn how to make us well when we're sick and don't seem to know how to *keep* us healthy. Mine tsk-tsked over my bruises and canker sores, but not one knew what to suggest. So finally it seemed I really had to do it myself.

I found that the fuel I needed to keep fighting fit while staying willowy, as swingy actresses should, was difficult to come by if you ate "American Normal," which was, nutritionally, what my life had been up to that point—high on junk and low on real goodies. My diet was loaded with sweets and more sweets. I grew up in orchardy California, but few of those sweets were the natural kind that grow on trees. Mostly they were hot fudge sundaes, home-made fudge, caramel chews, chocolate sodas—the gamut. I can remember a thousand long afternoons at double features fortified by candy bars and boxes of caramel corn. Any reward for work well done was more sweets. Trips to the dentist—and they were agonizingly frequent—were topped off with a nice big gooey triple-decked banana split eaten immediately afterward at the downstairs soda fountain. Later Mother would bake her fantastic rum cheese pie. (So that my darling mother doesn't think I'm picking on her, I must say that *all* my friends' mothers did the same thing, and as I look around wherever I go, I see kids today living on sugar, just as I used to do. Practically every kid I see in a restaurant has a soft drink in front of him, which is practically *all* sugar. It really amazes me how few drink milk.)

I was the best friend any ol' germ ever had. I always seemed to be getting something, and the first hint of recovery was greeted with—you guessed it!—a multilayered devil's food cake with inch-thick chocolate butter-cream frosting.

About 100,000,000 empty calories later I was a TV actress guest-starring in the likes of "Bonanza" and "Gunsmoke," and not even caring if those flashing smiles revealed hidden glints of gold—after all, everybody else had 'em. (My brother and I willed the gold in our teeth to each other when we were kids.)

For a while I exuded something generally regarded as enormous energy, but which I now recognize to have been mostly nerves—nudged by much nicotine and coffee. Then when I met Adelle Davis via her book, she made such good sense I really latched on. I'm extremely logical and everything you'll read in this book is logical. Everything makes good sense and nothing is foisted upon you with a "just do it." I've personally experimented with every-thing here and it really works!

Now the vitamin-brimming, high-prote, low-cal mix is a difficult bag to get into. So I decided early that if I were going to keep my actressy dimensions and produce real energy, I'd have to learn all about the hard-core nutrients and trip gingerly around the starch-sugar-fat pitfalls. Also, being a no-meat eater (meat's complete prote, but I've got a thing about animals) can complicate matters.

So I started visiting Farmer's Market in Los Angeles and a couple of health-food stores, and stocked my fridge and pantry shelves. Again I never cooked "by the book." From the start I improvised, and things came up tasting groovy. I'd smack my lips and say, "Hey, pretty smooth." Friends came to dine and turned my head by inviting themselves back. I remember one charmer who burned his kitchen eyes into me and intoned, "Naura baby, anytime you want you can put your sandals under my stove." I was barefoot at the time, so I loaded him up with Vitamin A to improve his vision.

I became a girl with a rep. Everybody was flipping over my meals. People would call and ask slyly, "Is it true you're putting out?" Meals, *si*, recipes, no.

Then I moved to New York to do some TV shows and decided for fun to open, in the shadow of Lincoln Center, a café called Opera Espresso. The restaurant was, as they say in show biz, an overnight sensation, a sleeper. The menu featured a lot of things I'd been trying out on my buddies on the Coast, but I still wouldn't give out the recipes.

The Opera Espresso grew into a monster that threatened to devour the actress, so when a terrific film offer out of the country materialized, I closed it, but with a heart that weighed a ton. Looking back on almost two years of juggling TV appearances and "Thoup" (a house specialty), I think it was one of the happiest times of my life. The success of the Opera Espresso was a loud yea for my fun-with-food attitude.

But besides having fun, once you open your mind to nutrition, all kinds of good things will begin to happen for you. You'll be astounded how much more you'll be able to do and how seldom you'll get tired. The way to build great health is with complete protein, and when I discovered it, things really began to improve.

There are two kinds of protein—complete and incomplete. Both consist of amino acids, and there are 22 in all. Eight of these amino acids the body can't synthesize; we get them only in our food. Incomplete protein contains some of the amino acids but not the essential eight. This book is concerned only with complete protein.

The best sources of complete protein are eggs, milk, yogurt, cheeses, wheat germ, powdered yeast, noninstant powdered milk, soybeans, sunflower seeds, sesame seeds, meat, fish, and fowl. Certain nuts, beans, peas, vegetables, fruits, and grains contain incomplete protein.

Throughout life, body proteins are broken down by enzymes in our cells. Unless enough complete protein is eaten, the cells are not all replaced. The less important body tissues are destroyed to free amino acids needed to rebuild the more vital tissues. You continue to function, but less and less well, until finally you start to fall apart. Not all at once. First a saggy muscle or two, then slumpy posture and perhaps jumpy nerves. In other words, without enough complete protein, we start to look and feel old. If this happened quickly, one would be panic stricken and try to save his body. But because it's slow, and because we accept old age and illness as part of life, few people use logic to see the cause and effect of nutrition and health.

Science has proved that many signs considered standard for old age are merely disease symptoms. Children of eight or ten with scurvy, (Vitamin C deficiency) lose their teeth, have humped-over shoulders, and saggy, wrinkly skin. Take a look at photos of scurvied kids and you'll see what I mean. They honestly look like old, old midgets—it's incredible. So we don't "grow" old—it's starving our cells of protein and necessary vitamins that stops them from growing and renewing themselves.

You may think you get plenty of protein every day. But if you eat two eggs, toast, and coffee for breakfast, a hamburger and coffee for lunch, and an average slice of roast beef with potatoes, vegetable, salad, and dessert for dinner, you may be astounded to learn you will get only 39 grams of complete protein for the day.

According to the Food and Nutrition Board in Washington, D.C., an average 5 foot 9 inch, 154-pound *healthy* man needs 70 grams of protein a day, and an average 5 foot 4 inch, 128-pound *healthy* woman needs 60 grams, and an average 5 foot 8 inch, 134-pound *healthy* teen-age boy needs 85 grams of protein a day. They don't tell you what a less-than-perfectly-healthy person needs—and let's face it, are most people really bursting with health? And how about those of us who are taller or heavier than average? Even perfectly healthy persons, in my opinion, all need much more than these minimum amounts. (The same board in Washington says that the minimum amount of Vitamin C is 70 mg. a day, yet Nobel prize winner Linus Pauling says that 3,000 mg. a day should probably be the minimum. I've been taking 6,000 mg. a day for several years, and I feel *great.* I haven't been sick or had a cold. Sometimes I up the C to 15,000 mgs. or more a day if I feel the touch of a virus or a strange ache.)

So you can see that Washington's protein figure can be very low. I get 40 grams of prote a day with yeast alone, and drink a quart of milk for 32 grams more. That's 72 grams right *there.* Then with eggs, cheese, and other high-prote foods, I usually end up with at least 125 or sometimes 150 grams every day.

Since I started really making an effort to feel healthy, all my old complaints have disappeared—I feel sensational right around the calendar. The disappointments and frustrations and ego-slapping confrontations that one meets head-on in life, and in show biz in particular, throw me not one little bit anymore. Nothing gets me down—for longer then ten seconds. Most of the time I'm on a natural, long-playing "high." "You must be taking something," people are always saying. "I'm taking a *lot,*" I hasten to agree. And that gives me the opening to go into my number on proper nutrition.

All the recipes in this book are superhigh in prote (to keep your batteries charged), low in calories (you won't miss those fattening sweets and starches, honest!), and easy to whip up. The amounts of protein grams are listed and the number of calories too. But forget the calories; memorize the protein content of milk, eggs, yeast, cottage cheese, etc., and you'll never have to worry about calories again. If you're loaded with prote, there just isn't room for anything unhealthful or fattening, and the extra energy you'll have will help to melt off any unwanted pounds.

All the recipes are originals and each passes the delectability test—food is *not* medicine. First things first—food has to grab our taste buds before we give a damn whether it's good for us.

Cook, eat, and *love* in superhealth, high heart—and high prote!

The Hip,
High-Prote, Low-Cal,
Easy-Does-It
Cookbook

1

Dynamite for Breakfast

BLAST OFF WITH ENERGY THAT LASTS ALL DAY LONG

GOOD MORNING, Sunshine. Good morning, Raindrops. Good morning, MORNING! WOW! And you *will* feel this great, too. If you had a gorgeous $25,000 Rolls or Maseratti, would you *dream* of going for a spin without making sure there was enough oil so the motor wouldn't be ruined? Of course not. And you'd never turn the key of your gorgeous Honda 750 on an empty tank. It needs gas to run on, right? So how awful to take that gorgeous body of yours (well, it *will* be gorgeous if you'll pay some attention to it) and think *your* motor can go, and *your* body can run, if you get up, slosh down some hot coffee to wake it up, down a greasy jelly donut, then guzzle more hot coffee to stimulate it and get it going.

1

Somebody's got to say, "But all I do is sit behind a desk all day —what do I *need* to eat better for?" Well, who says you have to sit behind that desk and just vegetate—feel awful and sluggish a lot of the time. What would happen if you woke up really hungry ('cause you didn't stuff yourself last night), and laid into some real goodies loaded with protein and low on calories? You might have so much energy you'd decide to walk to work instead of taking the bus. After all, that new energy's got to go *someplace.* Or maybe you'll start thinking about getting a bike and pedaling to work. Just think, fewer buses, fewer cars, fewer fumes—FWHEW!

Okay, let's move on to a *right* breakfast, one that'll wipe away the cobwebs and get the juices flowing.

Start with powdered yeast. It doesn't taste great, but whatta way to start the day. The results are so fabulous that *nothing* could stop me from taking it every day of my life. It will release all the nervous tension that you take for granted as part of a "now life." This tension is just trapped energy in your muscles and when released will become constructive energy. I absolutely guarantee that anyone who'll take this will feel more relaxed and have more energy and feel better in every way, mentally and physically. How can you beat that? A personal guarantee. But you can't do it hit and miss—it has to be *every day.*

Powdered yeast is all protein, no fat. (Don't take solid, un-cooked baker's yeast by mistake.) Powdered yeast has more B vitamins and more all-around nourishment than any other food. Two heaping tablespoonfuls have 20 grams of perfect, complete protein, which is as much as an average serving of beef. Yeast is probably the best-known food for beautifying the skin, and I don't know a man or woman, young or old, who wouldn't give a lot for great skin. Yeast is a fabulous way to diet. Take it just before dinner and you won't overeat—you'll push the mashed 'taters away 'cause you'll be *stuffed!* But start out verrry slowly—usually a person deficient in the B vites (as almost everybody is) has incomplete digestion. In a few days you'll have absorbed enough B's from the yeast so you can take more and more. Take ½ teaspoonful for the first three days (mixed with orange juice or defizzed no-cal soda if you're a little tubby), 1 teaspoonful the second three days, till you've worked up to 2 heaping tablespoonfuls in the morning and 2 at night. After ten days you'll need a pilot's license, 'cause you'll be flyin' and *then* you'll start sayin', "Good morning, MORNING!"

'Nuff said about yeast. Now for a breakfast to sink your teeth into. After the yeast, bite into Breakfast Cake Go-Go hot out of the oven and you may faint from happiness. Each slice gives you 17 grams of perfect, complete protein and only 329 calories—it's crunchy, chewy, and out of this world. You'll wonder how you ever managed to swallow those greasy donuts.

Apple Fritters are another groovy way to greet the day—crispy on the outside and melty on the inside, with little chunks of apple. Each one has 8 grams of protein and only 127 calories. Add a glass of skim milk and you've got 17 grams of prote and 217 cals.

I love milk, and every morning I put a teaspoon of Sanka or Postum in a cup of hot skim milk—tastes like *café au lait* or *café con leche caliente,* but no phony stimulant. By the way, calcium can't be absorbed by the body without some oil or fat with it, so use skim milk only when you're having something else with oil or fat in it. Every recipe in this book uses vegetable oil, so skim milk's okay.

(And speaking of vegetable oil, it's really fabulous for you. It's the principal source of the essential fatty acids we need for glossy hair, healthy hormones, a good sex life, and even for a diet. Lots of people think they're fat, but they're only waterlogged, and 2 tablespoons of vegetable oil a day will allow the excess water to leave the body. Each tablespoon of oil has 125 calories, but they'll help to keep you from feeling hungry for a long time. Always refrigerate vegetable oil once it's opened. And *never* use mineral oil for anything to do with the body—don't swallow it or use it as a body oil. It absorbs Vitamins A, D, E, and K and then washes them out of the body.)

Back to food. Try the Popovers with some of the sauces in

Chapter 7: Orange Marmalade Sauce or Lemony Sauce, or even Raisin Yogurt Dressing. Each Popover has 7 grams of prote and 148 cals, but add 2 tablespoons of Orange Marmalade Sauce and you get almost 4 grams of extra prote and only 78 cals—and it's a perfect combination. It's better for you than calorie-ful, protein-less jam any day, and it even *tastes* better!

Wonder Waffles are golden brown, crispy, and wonderful. If you like waffles (I love 'em) you'll really go for these. And Chapter 7 has some terrific toppings and syrups. Each waffle has 16 grams of prote and 339 cals.

And how about the Hangover Heavenly—the be-all to end all hangovers. It'll stop the buzzing and the butterflies and help pull you together. As George Ade said in "Remorse" in 1903:

A dark brown taste, a burning thirst,
A head that's ready to split and burst,
No time for mirth, no time for laughter,
The cold gray dawn of the morning after.

Poor Georgie could have used a Hangover Heavenly. Sounds like he was hung from the chandelier by his toes. It's a good idea to make it the night before so it'll be all ready when your shaky little hand reaches for it. Each glass has 22 grams of prote and 433 cals.

If you need a quickie breakfast, bake your Breakfast Cake Go-Go on Sunday, or some night when you're free, and freeze it. Then you can cut a big slab and stick it under the broiler while you're putting on your shoes or combing your locks. Or make your Apple Fritter batter the night before and just fry 'em in the morning. Or when you make waffles, use the leftover batter to make extra waffles and freeze 'em. You'll know the fridge is loaded with easy-does-it, high-prote, low-cal yummies that are ready in minutes!

And if you're *really* racing the clock, how about making one of the *sensational* lip-smackin' drinkin' delights like Marvy Mocha —it'll open your eyes and keep 'em sparklin' all day. Can you believe you'll get 28 grams of perfect, complete protein and only 394 calories, and it'll take all of about three minutes to make and drink?

Now, on to the recipes, so you can begin to blast-off all your days with Dynamite for Breakfast!

Breakfast Cake Go-Go

½ cup soy powder
½ cup soy grits
½ cup noninstant powdered skim milk
½ cup wheat germ (untoasted)
½ cup whole wheat flour
1 cup sunflower seeds
½ cup sesame seeds
2⅔ teaspoons granulated sugar substitute
½ teaspoon sea salt
3 eggs
½ cup skim milk
2 tablespoons safflower oil
2 tablespoons honey
1 cup fresh fruit (berries, apples, apricots, pears, peaches, etc.)

Combine soy powder, soy grits, powdered skim milk, wheat germ, whole wheat flour, sunflower seeds, sesame seeds, sugar substitute, and sea salt. In a separate bowl beat eggs into skim milk, then add safflower oil and honey. Mix well. Pour this into dry mixture and mix well. Add fruit and blend thoroughly. Pour batter into teflon-lined loaf pan and bake at 350° for 45 minutes or until golden brown on top. *Makes 10 slices.*

Each slice has
17 grams of complete protein
329 calories

Apple Crunch Pancakes

½ cup whole wheat flour
¼ cup wheat germ (untoasted)
½ cup soy powder
¼ cup soy grits
¼ teaspoon sea salt
1⅓ teaspoons granulated sugar substitute
6 eggs
2 cups skim milk
1 tablespoon safflower oil in skillet per pancake
2 ripe apples, chopped
2 tablespoons honey
1 teaspoon cinnamon

Mix whole wheat flour, wheat germ, soy powder, soy grits, sea salt, and sugar substitute. Beat eggs and blend into flour mixture. Add milk until batter is thin and smooth. Cover skillet bottom with safflower oil. When hot, pour in 5 tablespoons of batter. Tilt pan to spread batter and let cook one minute. Cover pancake with apples, a little honey and cinnamon. Pour 5 tablespoons batter over apples. Turn cake with wide pancake turner when brown on bottom. Brown other side. Serve folded over or roll loosely.   *Makes 4 pancakes.*

Each pancake has
28 grams of complete protein
485 calories

Banana Loaf

2 eggs
4 tablespoons safflower oil
2 medium ripe bananas
3 tablespoons honey
½ cup whole wheat pastry flour
¼ cup wheat germ (untoasted)
¾ cup soy powder
½ cup noninstant powdered skim milk
3⅓ teaspoons granulated sugar substitute
½ teaspoon sea salt

Mix eggs, oil, bananas, and honey in blender for 1 minute. In a large bowl mix whole wheat pastry flour, wheat germ, soy powder, powdered skim milk, sugar substitute, and sea salt. Pour in liquid mixture and blend well. Pour into teflon-lined loaf pan and bake at 350° for 45 minutes or until golden brown.

Makes 10 slices.

Each slice has
8 grams of complete protein
195 calories

Whole Wheat Muffins

¾ cup whole wheat flour
¼ cup wheat germ (untoasted)
½ cup soy powder
1 cup buttermilk
1 egg
2 tablespoons safflower oil
¼ cup blackstrap molasses
½ cup raisins
½ teaspoon sea salt

Mix whole wheat flour, wheat germ and soy powder. Put everything else in blender for 1 minute. Pour into flour mixture and stir lightly. The batter will be slightly lumpy. Put 1 tablespoon of the mixture into each space of muffin tin and bake at 350° for 25 minutes. *Makes 18 muffins.*

Each muffin has
2 grams of complete protein
82 calories

Powerhouse Pancakes

¾ cup whole wheat flour
¼ cup wheat germ (untoasted)
½ cup soy powder
¼ cup noninstant powdered skim milk
½ cup sesame seeds
2 eggs
1 cup skim milk
¼ teaspoon tea salt
1 tablespoon safflower oil in skillet per batch

Mix whole wheat flour, wheat germ, soy powder, powdered skim milk, and sesame seeds in large bowl. Add eggs, milk, and sea salt and mix thoroughly. Put 1 tablespoon safflower oil in skillet for each batch of pancakes.

Makes 20 medium pancakes.

Each pancake has
6½ grams of complete protein
104 calories

Popovers 'n' Out

1 cup skim milk
¼ cup noninstant powdered skim milk
½ cup soy powder
2 eggs
2 tablespoons safflower oil
¾ cup whole wheat flour
¼ teaspoon sea salt

Put all ingredients in blender and mix for 1 minute. Pour into teflon-lined muffin pan. Bake at 400° for about 45 minutes, or until golden brown on top.   *Makes 8 popovers.*

Each popover has
7 grams of complete protein
148 calories

Cheesy Waffles

½ cup whole wheat flour
¼ cup wheat germ (untoasted)
1 cup soy powder
¼ cup noninstant powdered skim milk
½ teaspoon sea salt
3 eggs
1¼ cups skim milk
6 tablespoons safflower oil
8 tablespoons (½ cup) grated Cheddar cheese

Mix whole wheat flour, wheat germ, soy powder, powdered skim milk, and sea salt in large bowl. Separate eggs. Put egg yolks, milk, oil, and cheese in blender for 30 seconds. Pour over flour mixture, stirring till mixed. Beat egg whites till stiff and fold into mixture. Bake in hot waffle iron till crispy. (If you want to use a cheese sauce as a topping, add ½ cup chopped green peppers to sauce while cooking, and add protein and calorie count of sauce to waffle.)   *Makes 6 waffles.*

> Each waffle (without sauce) has
> 19 grams of complete protein
> 363 calories

Waffle Crunch

> ½ cup wheat germ (untoasted)
> ½ cup soy powder
> ½ cup noninstant powdered skim milk
> ½ cup soy grits
> ½ teaspoon sea salt
> 2⅔ teaspoons granulated sugar substitute
> ½ cup sesame seeds
> 3 eggs
> 1¼ cups skim milk
> 6 tablespoons safflower oil

Combine wheat germ, soy powder, powdered skim milk, soy grits, sea salt, sugar substitute, and sesame seeds in large bowl. Separate eggs. Put egg yolks, milk, and safflower oil in blender and mix for 30 seconds. Pour into dry mixture and mix well. Beat egg whites till stiff and fold into batter. Bake in hot waffle iron till golden brown and crispy.   *Makes 6 waffles.*

> Each waffle has
> 23 grams of complete protein
> 426 calories

Wonder Waffles

1 cup whole wheat flour
¼ cup wheat germ (untoasted)
¼ cup soy powder
½ cup noninstant powdered skim milk
½ teaspoon sea salt
2⅔ teaspoons granulated sugar substitute
3 eggs
1¼ cups skim milk
6 tablespoons safflower oil

Mix whole wheat flour, wheat germ, soy powder, powdered skim milk, sea salt, and sugar substitute in large bowl. Separate eggs. Blend in egg yolks, milk, and oil. Mix well. Beat egg whites till stiff and fold into batter. Bake in hot waffle iron till golden brown.   *Makes 6 waffles.*

Each waffle has
16 grams of complete protein
339 calories

Italian Pancakes

½ cup whole wheat flour
½ cup soy powder
1½ teaspoons sea salt
1 pound ricotta cheese
2 eggs
2 egg yolks
3 tablespoons yogurt
1 tablespoon safflower oil in skillet per batch
cinnamon

Mix whole wheat flour, soy powder, and sea salt. Blend in with ricotta cheese. Mix eggs, egg yolks, and yogurt and blend well with cheese mixture. Put 1 tablespoon safflower oil in skillet for each batch of pancakes. Sprinkle with cinnamon.

Makes 20 medium pancakes.

Each pancake has
6 grams of complete protein
64 calories

Apple Fritters

⅔ cup whole wheat flour
⅓ cup soy powder
¼ teaspoon sea salt
2⅔ teaspoons granulated sugar substitute
¼ cup apple juice
½ teaspoon vanilla
2 eggs
1 cup chopped apples
safflower oil

Combine whole wheat flour, soy powder, sea salt, and sugar substitute. Mix apple juice and vanilla into flour mixture. Separate eggs. Add egg yolks and mix well. Beat egg whites stiff and fold into batter. Stir fruit into batter. Drop spoonfuls into deep, hot safflower oil (at least ½ inch deep). Fry two to five minutes, depending on how crispy you want them. Drain on thick paper towel.

Makes about 8 fritters.

Each fritter has
8 grams of complete protein
127 calories

Orange Juliette

1 whole orange, peeled
2 eggs
1 heaping tablespoon soy powder
1 heaping tablespoon noninstant powdered skim
    milk
1 tablespoon honey
1 tablespoon safflower oil
pinch of ground cloves

Cut orange into small pieces. Put all ingredients in blender and mix for 1 minute. Pour into tall glass.

Makes 1 serving.

Each glass has
26 grams of complete protein
524 calories

Honey Almond Fritters

¼ cup whole wheat pastry flour
¼ cup soy powder
¼ cup noninstant powdered skim milk
½ cup chopped almonds
1 teaspoon granulated sugar substitute
⅓ teaspoon sea salt
1 tablespoon grated lemon peel
2 eggs
2 tablespoons honey
1 teaspoon almond extract
safflower oil

Mix whole wheat pastry flour, soy powder, powdered skim milk, chopped almonds, sugar substitute, and sea salt in large bowl. In a separate bowl mix lemon peel, eggs, honey, and almond extract. Pour this into dry mixture and blend well. Put ½ inch safflower oil in skillet and heat. When very hot, drop mixture by spoon and fry till golden brown. Drain on thick paper towel.

Makes 8 fritters (serves 4 people).

Each fritter has
9½ grams of complete protein
171 calories

Hangover Heavenly

½ cup tomato juice
1 cup yogurt
1 heaping tablespoon soy powder
1 heaping tablespoon noninstant powdered skim milk
2 tablespoons chopped onion
½ cup water cress
1 tablespoon safflower oil
⅛ teaspoon sea salt
⅛ teaspoon pepper
1 tablespoon Worcestershire sauce

Put all ingredients in blender and mix for 1 minute. Pour into tall glass.

Makes 1 serving.

Each glass has
22 grams of complete protein
433 calories

Banana Groovy

1 ripe banana
1½ cups skim milk
1 tablespoon safflower oil
1 egg
1 heaping tablespoon noninstant powdered skim
    milk
⅓ teaspoon granulated sugar substitute
1 heaping tablespoon soy powder
pinch of nutmeg

Put all ingredients in blender and mix for ½ minute. Pour into tall glass. *Makes 1 serving.*

Each glass has
34 grams of complete protein
554 calories

Apple-cot Nectar

1 cup apple juice
½ cup fresh apricot halves
1 egg
1 heaping tablespoon soy powder
1 heaping tablespoon noninstant powdered skim
    milk
1 tablespoon safflower oil

Put all ingredients in blender and mix for ½ minute. Pour into tall glass. *Makes 1 serving.*

Each glass has
20 grams of complete protein
509 calories

Cocoa-Prote

1 egg
1 cup skim milk
1 tablespoon safflower oil
1 heaping tablespoon soy powder
1 heaping tablespoon noninstant powdered skim
   milk
1 level tablespoon carob powder or 1 teaspoon cocoa
   (unsweetened)
⅓ teaspoon granulated sugar substitute

Put all ingredients in blender and mix for ½ minute. Pour into tall glass.   *Makes 1 serving.*

Each glass has
29 grams of complete protein
440 calories

Creamy Eggnog

1 egg
1½ cups skim milk
⅓ teaspoon granulated sugar substitute
½ teaspoon vanilla
⅛ teaspoon nutmeg
1 heaping tablespoon soy powder
1 tablespoon safflower oil
1 heaping tablespoon noninstant powdered skim
   milk
pinch of ground ginger

Put all ingredients in blender and mix for 1 minute. Pour into tall glass.   *Makes 1 serving.*

Each glass has
34 grams of complete protein
469 calories

Marvy Mocha

1½ *cups cold skim milk*
1 *heaping tablespoon noninstant powdered skim milk*
1 *heaping tablespoon soy powder*
⅓ *teaspoon granulated sugar substitute*
2 *teaspoons instant Sanka (or coffee)*
1 *tablespoon safflower oil*
⅛ *teaspoon cinnamon*

Put all ingredients in blender and mix for ½ minute. Pour into tall glass.   *Makes 1 serving.*

Each glass has
28 grams of complete protein
394 calories

Orange Groove

1 *6-ounce can frozen orange juice (undiluted)*
½ *cup water*
½ *cup shredded unsweetened coconut*

2 heaping tablespoons soy powder
2 heaping tablespoons noninstant powdered skim milk
2½ cups skim milk
2 eggs
2 tablespoons safflower oil

Put all ingredients in blender and mix for 1 minute. Pour into tall glasses.   *Makes 4 servings*

Each glass has
16 grams of complete protein
355 calories

Tomato Tomcat

1 cup tomato juice
½ cup skim milk cottage cheese
1 heaping tablespoon noninstant powdered skim milk
1 heaping tablespoon soy powder
1 tablespoon safflower oil
½ teaspoon soy sauce
pinch sea salt
pinch pepper
pinch basil

Put all ingredients in blender and mix for 1 minute. Pour into tall glass.   *Makes 1 serving.*

Each glass has
38 grams of complete protein
379 calories

Yummy Yogi

> 1 cup yogurt
> ½ cup skim milk
> 2 tablespoons frozen orange juice (undiluted)
> 1 heaping tablespoon soy powder
> 1 heaping tablespoon noninstant powdered skim milk
> 1 tablespoon safflower oil
> ¼ teaspoon allspice

Put all ingredients in blender and mix for 1 minute. Pour into tall glass. *Makes 1 serving.*

Each glass has
27 grams of complete protein
478 calories

2

Egg-o-mania

EGG-CITING NEW WAYS
TO FIX EGGS

I'M AN EGGSPERT—I love 'em. I'm also egg-o-centric—my life seems to revolve around 'em. They're one of the very best ways to get lots of protein and not many calories. In fact, the essential amino acids are supplied in greatest abundance in egg yolk and fresh milk. Ounce for ounce, each contains more complete protein than muscle meats such as steaks, roast beef, and chops.

I suppose some of you have heard that eggs aren't good for you because of the cholesterol in them. But you may not be aware of the high amount of lecithin in each egg yolk. Leci-what? Lecithin —less-i-thin, from the Greek word *likithos*, which means egg yolk. It emulsifies, or breaks up, all the cholesterol in the yolk, so eggs are *great* for you. The logical thing is not to stop eating all the other good things that contain cholesterol, but to add lecithin to the diet. Every morning I add 2 tablespoons of lecithin to my yeast, and the same at night. It has a nutty flavor, and 4 tablespoons a day is good. You don't have to begin slowly as you do with yeast—you can start right out with 4 tablespoons. Every cell in the body needs lecithin. It's also great for the skin and fantastic for your nerves.

Natural foods that contain fat (eggs are one) have a combination of lecithin-cholesterol, and the lecithin dissolves the cholesterol. Food processors and refiners mess around with nature and break up the combination. When they hydrogenate (harden) fats, as they do in shortenings, margarines, and cooking fats, the lecithin is discarded and all you have left is the cholesterol. Since most people eat refined and processed food, it's no wonder lots of them have cholesterol problems. We ought to sue for robbery —the lecithin has been *stolen* from us!

I honestly don't miss even a little eating meat, and one of the reasons is eggs. You can have a ball with 'em. They can be prepared in so many styles, it's like a tour around the world. I fix 'em *à la* every country I've ever lived in and a few I haven't.

When you try Eggs Argentine, you'll flip out. Put on a little tango music, imagine you're sitting in a *confiteria* (literally sweet shop, but like a coffee house), and you'll be transported to that beautiful country. I lived there almost two years while making an American film, and even though it's known as the Beef Capital of the World, I loved my Eggs Argentine and got lots of the natives hooked on 'em. Each serving gives you a whopping 32 grams of prote and only 424 cals.

And how about Madame Curried Eggs—oriental with a French flair. Eggs are served in a rich and creamy sauce, but with hardly any calories—only 325 a serving, and of course that's a whole meal. It's hard to believe that something so rich tasting has 24 grams of complete protein, which is more than the average serving of steak would give you.

The Swiss Egg Cakes will melt in your mouth. They're as easy to make as pancakes, only they taste a lot different. If you like Swiss cheese, you'll love these. Each one has 18 grams of prote and only 232 cals—a bargain at any price!

Sometime flip on Tchaikowsky and whip up the Russian Eggs —they're festive and fun (if you dig caviar). You'll get 35 grams of prote and 509 cals.

And of course you'll find a few soufflés, which are really quite easy to make—they just take a while to bake. You can pop the Onion Soufflé in the oven and go about making a salad and setting the table while it's baking. It's worth the time 'cause it's divine. If you serve it as a side dish with something else as entrée, you'll get four servings at 10 grams of prote and 219 cals each, but if it's your main course for two people, double those figures for 20 grams of prote and 438 calories.

Even my dog Morris loves eggs. At nine pounds, with a shaggy, un-poodly haircut, he eats one mixed with dry dog food and it fills him up. For some unknown reason he likes eggs, milk, soybeans, and cottage cheese better than meat. (I've always thought that animals became like their owners—but maybe it's the other way around!) Of course Morris gets his daily yeast, lecithin, and vites —after all, I'd like him to live as long as I do. His predecessor, Maurice Chevalier II, whom I'd had since I was a kid, lived to be nineteen (a record for a poodle), and right to the last, people would ask if he were a puppy—honest! Only in his last years did he get health food, but it really worked!

Now that you know how terrific eggs are for you, here are the recipes, so you can become an egg-o-maniac too!

Eggs-otic

4 eggs
½ cup cottage cheese with chives
1 heaping tablespoon noninstant powdered skim milk
2 tablespoons sesame seeds
⅛ teaspoon basil
⅛ teaspoon cardomom seed
⅛ teaspoon ginger
½ teaspoon sea salt
⅛ teaspoon pepper
2 tablespoons safflower oil

Put eggs in blender. Add cottage cheese and powdered skim milk. Blend for 30 seconds. Add sesame seeds and all spices for another 10 seconds. Put safflower oil in large skillet and scramble egg mixture over very low flame.   *Makes 2 servings*

Each serving has
28 grams of complete protein
450 calories

Swiss Egg Cakes

¼ cup whole wheat flour
¼ cup noninstant powdered skim milk
¼ cup soy powder
1 teaspoon sea salt
1⅓ teaspoons granulated sugar substitute
1 cup skim milk
4 eggs
¼ cup diced Swiss cheese
2 tablespoons safflower oil

Mix together flower, powdered skim milk, soy powder, sea salt, and sugar substitute. Add milk, Swiss cheese, and eggs and beat well. Put 2 tablespoons safflower oil in large skillet and pour ¼ of batter in. Sauté on both sides till browned. Use rest of batter the same way. *Makes 4 servings.*

Each serving has
18 grams of complete protein
232 calories

Eggs Parisiens

4 eggs
1 heaping tablespoon noninstant powdered skim
    milk
2 tablespoons Roquefort cheese
4 tablespoons finely chopped onion
4 tablespoons finely chopped chive
2 tablespoons finely chopped parsley
⅛ teaspoon marjoram
½ teaspoon sea salt
⅛ teaspoon thyme
¼ teaspoon pepper
2 tablespoons safflower oil

Beat eggs and powdered skim milk in a large bowl. Add cheese, onion, chive, and parsley and beat well. Add seasonings and mix in. Put oil in skillet and heat. Pour in egg mixture and scramble slowly over very low flame. *Makes 2 servings.*

Each serving has
18 grams of complete protein
251 calories

Greek Eggs

4 eggs
½ cup feta cheese
4 black oily olives, chopped
1 heaping tablespoon noninstant powdered skim milk
¼ teaspoon chervil
2 tablespoons safflower oil

Put eggs, cheese, olives, and powdered skim milk in blender. Mix for 30 seconds. Add chervil and blend a few seconds more. Put safflower oil in skillet and heat. Pour egg mixture into skillet and scramble over very low flame.   *Makes 2 servings.*

Each serving has
26 grams of complete protein
390 calories

Eggs Florentine

4 eggs, hard-boiled
2 cups cooked spinach
1 cup Creamy Cream Sauce (Chapter 7)
½ cup grated Parmesan cheese
4 tablespoons wheat germ (untoasted)

Cut eggs in half, lengthwise. Lay spinach on bottom of casserole, then place eggs on spinach. Pour on heated sauce and sprinkle on cheese. Top it all with wheat germ. Brown for few minutes in preheated 450° oven.   *Makes 4 servings*

Each serving has
21 grams of complete protein
298 calories

Mexican Eggs

4 eggs
6 tablespoons finely chopped onions
¼ cup finely chopped green pepper
1 small tomato
½ large avocado
½ teaspoon chili powder
1 heaping tablespoon noninstant powdered skim
    milk
dash Tabasco
1 tablespoon safflower oil

Put eggs, onions, and green pepper in blender and mix for 10 seconds. Cut up tomato and avocado and add. Put chili powder, powdered skim milk and Tabasco in blender and mix everything for 20 seconds. Put oil in skillet and heat over low flame. Pour in egg mixture and scramble very slowly.

Makes 2 servings.

Each serving has
16 grams of complete protein
379 calories

Oriental Eggs

4 eggs
¾ cup finely chopped onions
¾ cup finely chopped green peppers
1 cup fresh bean sprouts
½ teaspoon sea salt
1 tablespoon soy sauce
1 heaping tablespoon noninstant powdered skim
    milk
1 heaping tablespoon soy powder
2 tablespoons safflower oil

Mix all ingredients (except oil) well. Put safflower oil in a large skillet, then drop mixture from a tablespoon to form little pancakes. Sauté on both sides till browned.

Makes 2 servings.

Each serving has
19 grams of complete protein
288 calories

Eggs Argentine

4 eggs
½ cup skim milk cottage cheese
¼ cup grated Cheddar cheese
1 heaping tablespoon noninstant powdered skim
    milk
⅛ teaspoon basil
¼ cup chopped green peppers
2 tablespoons safflower oil

Put eggs, cottage cheese, Cheddar cheese, pow-
dered skim milk, and basil in blender and mix for 20 seconds. Pour
oil into skillet and add mixture plus green peppers. Scramble
slowly over very low flame. *Makes 2 servings.*

Each serving has
32 grams of complete protein
424 calories

Eggs-in-a-Basket

2 tablespoons safflower oil
8 slices American cheese
4 eggs
½ teaspoon sea salt
¼ teaspoon cayenne pepper
1 tablespoon chives
1 tablespoon chopped onion
1 tablespoon catsup
1 teaspoon Worcestershire sauce

Into a teflon-lined muffin pan put ½ teaspoon oil
in each of four spaces. Then put 2 slices of cheese at the bottom
of each space. Break 1 egg into each space. Mix together seasonings, chives, onion, catsup, and Worcestershire sauce and pour
over eggs. Bake in oven at 350° about 15 minutes or until firm.
Makes 2 servings.

Each serving has
28 grams of complete protein
580 calories

Russian Eggs

4 eggs
2 heaping tablespoons noninstant powdered skim
    milk
½ cup skim milk
2 tablespoons safflower oil
4 tablespoons caviar
4 tablespoons chopped onions

Separate eggs. Mix yolks with powdered skim milk and skim milk. Beat whites till stiff and fold into mixture. Pour oil into large skillet, add mixture, and cook over very low flame. Do not scramble. When top is dry, lift out with spatula onto large platter. Spoon caviar and onions onto omelet and fold over. Cut into 2 pieces. *Makes 2 servings.*

Each serving has
35 grams of complete protein
509 calories

Onion Soufflé

3 eggs
6 onions, chopped
2 heaping tablespoons soy powder
1 cup skim milk
1 tablespoon Worcestershire sauce
1 teaspoon soy sauce
½ teaspoon sea salt
¼ teaspoon pepper
¼ teaspoon rosemary
2 tablespoon safflower oil

Separate eggs. Mix yolks, onions, soy powder, skim milk, Worcestershire sauce, soy sauce, sea salt, pepper, and rosemary. Beat egg whites till stiff and fold into onion mixture. Turn into casserole rubbed with safflower oil and bake at 300° for 45 minutes or until brown on top.   *Makes 2 servings.*

Each serving has
20 grams of complete protein
438 calories

Eggs Mardi Gras

4 eggs
½ cup cottage cheese with chives
1 heaping tablespoon noninstant powdered skim
    milk
2 tablespoons safflower oil
1 tomato, chopped
1 clove garlic, chopped
⅛ teaspoon basil
½ teaspoon sea salt
squirt Tabasco
¼ teaspoon pepper

Beat eggs into cottage cheese until well mixed. Add powdered skim milk, oil, and tomato and blend thoroughly. Add all other ingredients, mixing after each addition. Pour into large skillet and scramble slowly over very low flame.

Makes 2 servings.

Each serving has
26 grams of complete protein
383 calories

Eggplant Soufflé

1 eggplant
¼ cup wheat germ (untoasted)
¼ cup soy powder
2 tablespoons safflower oil
1 onion, chopped
½ teaspoon sea salt
¼ teaspoon pepper
½ teaspoon coriander seed
2 eggs
¾ cup skim milk
2 heaping tablespoons noninstant powdered skim milk

Wash whole unpeeled eggplant and place in baking dish. Bake for 45 minutes at 400°. Peel, and mash eggplant. Combine eggplant, wheat germ, soy powder, oil, onion, sea salt, pepper, and coriander seed. Separate eggs. Combine yolks, milk, and powdered skim milk and stir into eggplant mixture. Beat egg whites till stiff and fold into mixture. Turn into casserole rubbed with safflower oil. Bake at 300° for 45 minutes.

Makes 4 servings

Each serving has
13 grams of complete protein
219 calories

Cheesy Brown Rice Souffle

4 eggs
¼ cup cooked brown rice
¼ cup finely chopped onion
¾ cup skim milk
½ teaspoon sea salt
1 tablespoon Worcestershire sauce
dash Tabasco
¼ teaspoon paprika
2 tablespoons safflower oil
1 cup grated carrot
¼ cup noninstant powdered skim milk
¼ cup soy powder
1 cup grated American cheese

Separate eggs. In a large pan, mix egg yolks, rice, onion, skim milk, salt, Worcestershire sauce, Tabasco, paprika, oil, and grated carrot. Bring to boil, stirring constantly. Add powdered skim milk, soy powder, and grated cheese and keep stirring till cheese is melted. Remove from heat. Beat egg whites till stiff. Fold beaten whites into cheese mixture and pour into 1-quart baking dish which has been rubbed with safflower oil. Bake at 300° for 45 minutes or until brown on top.

Makes 4 servings.

Each serving has
23 grams of complete protein
363 calories

Madame Curried Eggs

1 tablespoon safflower oil
1 heaping tablespoon noninstant powdered skim
    milk
1 heaping tablespoon soy powder
1 tablespoon chopped onion
½ teaspoon curry powder
¼ teaspoon sea salt
⅛ teaspoon cayenne pepper
1 cup skim milk
4 hard-cooked eggs, cut in quarters, lengthwise

Mix oil, powdered skim milk, soy powder, chopped onion, and seasonings. Slowly stir in milk, keeping mixture smooth. Cook over low heat, stirring till thickened. Add eggs and simmer for 5 minutes, or until warmed through.

Makes 2 servings.

Each serving has
24 grams of complete protein
325 calories

Roman Eggs

4 eggs
¼ teaspoon oregano
2 tablespoons chopped onion
4 chopped pimiento-stuffed green olives
1 heaping tablespoon noninstant powdered skim
    milk
2 tablespoons safflower oil
½ cup mozzarella cheese

Put eggs, oregano, onion, olives, and powdered skim milk in blender and mix for 20 seconds. Into two glass baking (custard) cups, put oil. Pour egg mixture into cups and top with cut-up pieces of cheese. Bake in oven at 350° about 20 minutes or until firm and cheese is melty.   *Makes 2 servings.*

Each serving has
26 grams of complete protein
389 calories

3

Snappy-tizers

HIGH-PROTE PARTY WAYS
TO BEGIN A MEAL

IF YOU FEEL TERRIFIC, you'll like yourself. If you like yourself, you'll like people. If you like people, you'll want to give 'em the very best you've got. The next time you're going to entertain a few pals and want the best for them, these appetizers will wow 'em. They look and taste great, are all terrifically nutritious—and so different. Every one is original and a real grabber. And after you're tried these, try concocting some of your own. It's really fun. As long as the ingredients are all high prote and low cal, you'll come up with some real winners.

The Fried Cheese 'n' Chili Balls are so special people flip over them. Serve 'em hot and you'll hear raves into next week. Each ball has 4 grams of protein and only 53 calories. But make plenty, 'cause they go fast!

You might put another skillet on the fire and make the Sesame-Cheese Balls to give your friends a choice. When you say "Have a ball," you'll mean it. Each one has 3 grams of prote and 51 cals.

If you're into dips, try the Smashed Eggplant Dip. It's really different in an Armenian way. At the same party serve Chili Con Queso Dip and Mozzarella Peppers. You'll have a "trip" with no drugs, no expense, no packing, hardly any calories, and lots and lots of complete protein. In fact, these appetizers are so filling and so high in prote that they actually can be a whole meal. Set a few of them on a buffet table and forget dinner. Five Cheese 'n' Chili Balls have 20 grams of prote, the same as an average serving of steak, and 265 cals. Five Sesame Cheese Balls have 15 grams of prote and 255 cals. The dips are the same. Two tablespoons of Chili Con Queso Dip will have 4 grams of prote and 50 cals. So put a large salad bowl of greens on your buffet table with a couple of choices of high-prote, low-cal dressings and a loaf of Molasses Nut Bread (Chapter 8). You really don't have to worry about anything else for dinner. It's like eating at Farmer's Market in Los Angeles, which is one of my favorite "trips." You pick out one thing at one booth, something else at another, until you've got four or five dishes, then find a vacant table and chair and have a variety feast. Never a dull dish. And of course lots of groovy atmosphere (that you gotta do on your own).

Another idea that's good and filling and good for you is to use raw vegetables with your dips instead of crackers and chips. Clean a bunch of raw carrots and slice lengthwise, then cut some raw cauliflower into little pieces and stick toothpicks in 'em, get some cherry tomatoes, brussels sprouts, and fresh mushrooms and spear them with toothpicks, cut fresh green peppers into long strips and start dunkin'. Of course you can use celery and scallions too. A plate all fixed up with different colored vegetables all around a bowl of dip really has a festive look, and you're getting all the high prote in the dip and the low cal of the vegetables.

When you toast *"à votre santé,"* you'll really mean it!

Fried Cheese 'n' Chili Balls

1 cup grated Parmesan cheese
1 cup skim milk cottage cheese
2 egg yolks
2 tablespoons chili powder
1 teaspoon sea salt
1 teaspoon paprika
2 heaping tablespoons noninstant powdered skim
    milk
2 tablespoons wheat germ (untoasted)
1 heaping tablespoon soy powder
¼ cup safflower oil

Mix Parmesan cheese, cottage cheese, egg yolks, chili powder, sea salt, paprika, and powdered skim milk in a bowl. Blend thoroughly. Form tiny balls, about 1 inch in diameter. In a separate bowl blend wheat germ and soy powder. Roll each cheese ball in dry mixture, coating completely. Fry in hot safflower oil in large skillet until golden brown.

Makes 30 cheese balls.

Each cheese ball has
4 grams of complete protein
53 calories

Mozzarella Peppers

8 green peppers
1 pound mozzarella cheese
Sea salt
Pepper
1 clove garlic, minced
oregano

Cut peppers in half, seed and remove ribs. Cut mozzarella cheese into 16 pieces. Sprinkle salt and pepper inside each pepper half. Put cheese inside each pepper half and top with tiny pieces of garlic and a sprinkle of oregano. Put under low broiler flame for few minutes until pepper softens and cheese gets melty. Bring both halves of pepper together and fasten with a toothpick. *Makes 16 appetizers.*

Each appetizer has
8 grams of complete protein
99 calories

Potted Cheese Appetizer

1 cup grated American cheese
1 tablespoon safflower oil
½ teaspoon sea salt
½ teaspoon pepper
⅛ teaspoon cayenne pepper
½ teaspoon poppy seed
¼ teaspoon dry mustard
2 egg yolks
⅓ cup yogurt
2 heaping tablespoons noninstant powdered skim milk
1 heaping tablespoon soy powder

Melt cheese in oil and add seasonings. Stir in egg yolks and yogurt, then mix in powdered skim milk and soy powder. Simmer over low heat, stirring constantly until thick and smooth. Refrigerate. *Makes 1 ½ cups (24 tablespoons).*

Each tablespoon has
3 grams of complete protein
41 calories

Stuft Cucumbers

4 large cucumbers
½ cup cottage cheese with chives
½ cup sunflower seeds, chopped
1 tablespoon chopped pimiento
1 heaping tablespoon noninstant powdered skim
    milk
½ teaspoon sea salt
½ teaspoon pepper
½ teaspoon marjoram
¼ teaspoon paprika

Peel and core the cucumbers. Mix all other ingredients in bowl and stuff cucumbers. Refrigerate till ready to serve. Cut each cucumber into 10 slices.   *Makes 40 slices.*

Each slice has
3 grams of complete protein
15 calories

Cheese Roll-a-Teeny

8 slices American cheese
8 slices Swiss cheese
½ cup cottage cheese with chives
4 tablespoons chopped onion
1 teaspoon poppy seed
½ teaspoon dry mustard
¼ teaspoon sea salt
¼ teaspoon pepper

Lay out 8 slices American cheese. Put a slice of Swiss cheese over each one. Mix all other ingredients in bowl.

Spoon mixture onto cheese slices. Roll up and put 2 toothpicks to hold, one at each end. Broil under low flame for 10 minutes, then cut in half, each half having a toothpick to hold it together.

Makes 16 appetizers.

> Each appetizer has
> 10 grams of complete protein
> 137 calories

Fluff Puffs

> 2 heaping tablespoons soy powder
> 4 heaping tablespoons noninstant powdered skim milk
> ½ teaspoon sea salt
> 1 teaspoon paprika
> ¼ teaspoon pepper
> ½ teaspoon thyme
> 4 eggs
> 2 tablespoons minced onion
> ½ cup American cheese, diced
> ¼ cup safflower oil

Mix soy powder, powdered skim milk, sea salt, paprika, pepper and thyme. Add eggs and mix well. Add onion and cheese and continue mixing. Heat oil in large skillet and drop large spoons of mixture into hot oil, turning so each one is a golden brown. Makes 20 puffs, but if you like them smaller it makes many more.

Makes 20 puffs.

> Each puff has
> 4 grams of complete protein
> 73 calories

Chili Con Queso Dip

3 cups yogurt
½ cup grated Cheddar cheese
1 cup grated jack cheese
½ cup noninstant powdered skim milk
½ cup soy powder
4 tablespoons minced onion
1 clove garlic, minced
1 tablespoon safflower oil
1 teaspoon sea salt
1 teaspoon paprika
1 tablespoon chili powder
½ teaspoon Tabasco sauce

Put yogurt and both cheeses in pan over very low heat. Add powdered skim milk and soy powder. Mix well. Add onion, garlic, oil, sea salt, paprika, chili powder and Tabasco sauce, blending thoroughly.   *Makes 4 cups.*

Each cup has
29 grams of complete protein
400 calories

Marinated Eggplant Cubes

1 eggplant
2 cloves garlic
1 teaspoon sea salt
½ cup cider vinegar
½ teaspoon black pepper
½ teaspoon basil
½ teaspoon oregano

4 tablespoons safflower oil
1 heaping tablespoon soy powder
2 heaping tablespoons noninstant powdered skim
   milk

Cut eggplant into cubes. Put on pie tin and bake in oven at 400° for about 30 minutes, or until done. In large bowl mash garlic with salt. Add vinegar and all seasonings. Put eggplant cubes in mixture and refrigerate overnight. To serve, stir in oil, soy powder, and powdered skim milk. Mix well. Stick toothpicks in each piece of eggplant.   *Makes 8 servings.*

Each serving has
3 grams of complete protein
101 calories

Sesame Cheese Balls

4 eggs
2 cups grated sharp Cheddar cheese
1 cup sesame seeds
¼ teaspoon sea salt
½ teaspoon paprika
½ teaspoon pepper
¼ teaspoon dry mustard
1 tablespoon Worcestershire sauce
2 heaping tablespoons soy powder
4 heaping tablespoons noninstant powdered skim
   milk
¼ cup safflower oil

Separate eggs. Beat whites till peaked. Add yolks, cheese, and sesame seeds. Beat well and add sea salt, paprika, pepper, mustard, and Worcestershire sauce. Slowly beat in soy powder and powdered skim milk. Form into small balls and fry in hot oil until golden brown.   *Makes 60 cheese balls.*

> Each cheese ball has
> 3 grams of complete protein
> 51 calories

Smashed Eggplant Dip

> 1 small eggplant
> ½ cup chopped black olives, preferably the oily, wrinkled kind
> 1 minced green pepper
> 1 minced onion
> 1 tablespoon safflower oil
> 1 tablespoon olive oil
> 1 heaping tablespoon soy powder
> 2 heaping tablespoons noninstant powdered skim milk
> ½ teaspoon sea salt
> ½ teaspoon pepper
> ¼ teaspoon turmeric

Cut eggplant into small pieces. Put on pie tin and bake at 350° for 30 minutes until tender. Peel when cool. Mash peeled eggplant with olives. Mix well with minced green peppers and onions. Add 2 oils, soy powder, and powdered skim milk. Serve cold.   *Makes 3 cups.*

> Each cup has
> 7 grams of complete protein
> 242 calories

4

There's a Tiger in My Thoup

EASY-DOES-IT ONE-DISH MEALS

THE OPERA ESPRESSO was the most adorable restaurant I've ever seen. It had a quaint old-world charm, and yet it was hip and sunny and musical. Two walls were windows overlooking Lincoln Center. Over a hundred growing plants filled window boxes, and the sun shining through them was glorious. I had begun taking yeast and lecithin a few months before and was brimming with energy, and decided I'd love to have my very own restaurant where I could use all my own recipes and have a "home away from home." I told my friends and they were all eager to help; it became a real do-it-yourself project. First, an old flower store was rented right across from Lincoln Center and we began decorating. All my buddies were there with paint scrapers and paint

45

brushes and hammers and nails, and the fun began—it really didn't even seem like work. We laid black and white vinyl squares on the floor, painted the walls yellow and the ceiling dark green, hung antique chandeliers and put in the window boxes. One friend brought her portable sewing machine and made seat covers for all the second-hand chairs I'd bought. Another refinished the table tops.

When the sidewalk café opened, it was the first year-round sidewalk café in New York history. I know, because the man at the license bureau told me I finally wore down his resistance (just the yeast working!). In summer it was surrounded by shrubs and hanging plants and fresh air. In winter it was Plexiglas enclosed with infrared heaters and a hothouse collection of plants and flowers. And every bit of this was do-it-yourself. Magazines and newspapers did full-page picture stories. At our opening night party I personally cooked over 600 appetizers for a gang of people. Everyone raved about the place. It was the hip place to be.

There are two reasons for going on like this about the Opera Espresso. First, I love to remember the fun of it, and second, I'm leading up to our house speciality, "Thoup." I used to make a very thick soup that everyone dug. I named it "Thoup," and it was a smash hit. I invented seven of them—one for each day. Then later I made up lots more.

Garden-Great Thoup has just about every vegetable, and of course you get all the vites and nutrition because you don't throw the liquid away. Each serving has 23 grams of protein and only 511 calories. (And remember, we don't count incomplete vegetable prote, only perfect complete prote.)

Cheese Thoup is made with Swiss cheese and its taste is so different it's a real grabber. You'll get 22 grams of prote and only a low 298 cals. Tomato Cheese Thoup is tangy and cheddary and has 16 grams of prote per serving and 322 calories.

You don't have to be Jewish to enjoy the Borscht Thoup, which is a terrific mixture of beets and other goodies you put in your blender for half a minute and then simmer for 15 minutes. It's easy to make and easy to eat, and you'll feel good knowing you're getting 15 grams of prote and only 266 cals. Add a green salad and you're all set.

You don't have to be Irish to dig into the Irish Rarebit. It's not "Thoup" but a one-dish meal made of Cheddar cheese that you can serve over No-Knead, Easy-Does-It Bread (Chapter 8) or anything else you feel like. Each serving of rarebit alone gives you 21 grams of prote and 351 cals.

Moving westward we come to the Old West Casserole, just like the cowboys fix up on the chuck wagon, only it's a lot more nourishing and a lot less fattening. You'll get 29 grams of prote and 480 cals.

Now we come to possibly the highest protein, least expensive food known to man—soybeans. They're loaded with perfect, complete protein. In fact, they have more than twice as much complete protein as the same amount of meat—any meat. They contain calcium and the B vites too, and they're sensational for diets because there's no fat and no starch, just pure prote. I can't figure out why so few people know about them and use them, but I'm out to help change that. They cost pennies per serving as against dollars for beef, and they're much more nourishing. So whenever you hear someone complain about meat prices, tell them about soybeans.

You can buy them canned, but why deal with preservatives? Soak one cup of dry soybeans in two cups of water in an ice tray for about an hour, then freeze them and keep them ready frozen for any dish you have in mind—just pop out as many cubes as you need. Unfrozen they need at least three hours' cooking time, but when frozen they need much less. I like them crunchy, so I cook them only a half hour or so, but if you like them softer, cook them longer until they're the consistency you like. You can cook them in other liquids than water: bouillon, tomato juice, soup stock. If you have stewed tomatoes, add some chopped onions, garlic, sea salt, and a few cubes of frozen soybeans, and you'll have a whole meal with high prote and low cals. If you like 'em sweet, add a little blackstrap molasses.

For a good snack take soybeans that have been soaked, frozen, and simmered a little. Put them into a skillet with a little safflower oil, cook for a few minutes till golden brown, and sprinkle with sea salt. I like them better than peanuts.

Soy grits are soybeans that have been broken up into little pieces. They cook in just minutes. Soy powder is the ground soybean. I use the beans, grits, and powder in lots of recipes. They don't have a strong flavor of their own, so they can be used in almost anything.

Learning the importance of soybeans can be a really tremendous discovery in your life. It was for me.

Garden-Great Thoup

4 large carrots
2 green peppers
4 large onions
1 cup fresh spinach
4 large zucchini
4 large tomatoes
1 clove garlic
2 cups water
2 tablespoons Worcestershire sauce
1 tablespoon soy sauce
2 teaspoons sea salt
1 teaspoon pepper
2 bay leaves
1 teaspoon celery seeds
½ teaspoon sage
1 cup soy grits
½ cup kasha
4 tablespoons wheat germ (untoasted)
¼ cup soy powder
2 tablespoons safflower oil

Cut carrots, green peppers, onions, spinach, zucchini, and tomatoes into chunks or small pieces. Mince garlic and add to vegetables. Put all vegetables in water and add Worcestershire sauce, soy sauce, sea salt, pepper, bay leaves, celery seeds, and sage, bring to a boil and then simmer for 30 minutes. Add soy grits, kasha, wheat germ, soy powder, and oil, mix well, and simmer another 20 minutes. *Makes 4 servings.*

Each serving has
23 grams of complete protein
511 calories

Cheese Thoup

1 cup water
1 cube or package vegetable bouillon
1 tablespoon Worcestershire sauce
1 teaspoon paprika
½ teaspoon sea salt
2 heaping tablespoons noninstant powdered skim
    milk
1 cup yogurt
4 tablespoons chopped onion
2 eggs
1 cup shredded Swiss cheese

Mix water, bouillon, Worcestershire sauce, paprika, sea salt, and powdered skim milk in large covered pan till smooth. Add yogurt and chopped onion. Beat eggs, add to mixture, and bring to a simmer. Add Swiss cheese and stir till melted. Simmer for 5 minutes. *Makes 4 servings.*

Each serving has
22 grams of complete protein
298 calories

Lemon Thoup

4 eggs
½ cup lemon juice
4 cups water
2 packages or cubes vegetable bouillon
½ teaspoon sea salt
¼ teaspoon pepper
2 heaping tablespoons soy powder
1 tablespoon safflower oil

Put eggs and lemon juice in blender for 30 seconds. Boil water and add vegetable bouillon, stirring until well mixed. Gradually add blended eggs and lemon juice, stirring until blended. Simmer for 3 minutes. Add sea salt, pepper, soy powder, and safflower oil and continue stirring for 3 more minutes until smooth and creamy. Serve either piping hot or chilled.

Makes 4 servings.

Each serving has
10 grams of complete protein
137 calories

Creamy Tomato Thoup

8 large ripe tomatoes
2 cups water
1 onion, chopped
1 teaspoon granulated sugar substitute
4 cloves
2 tablespoons safflower oil
¼ cup soy powder
⅔ cup noninstant powdered skim milk
⅛ teaspoon oregano
1 teaspoon sea salt
1 cup yogurt

Put tomatoes and water in large covered pot. Simmer for 10 minutes. Add onion, sugar substitute, cloves, and safflower oil. Slowly stir in soy powder and powdered skim milk until blended. Add oregano, sea salt, and yogurt. Simmer for 15 minutes.

Makes 4 servings.

Each serving has
14 grams of complete protein
269 calories

Groovy Egg Thoup

½ cup soy grits
1 cup water
1 cup tomato juice
2 tablespoons Worcestershire sauce
¼ cup soy powder
2 heaping tablespoons noninstant powdered skim
    milk
2 onions
4 tomatoes
1 green pepper
1 teaspoon sea salt
½ teaspoon pepper
½ teaspoon chili powder
¼ teaspoon paprika
2 tablespoons safflower oil
4 eggs

Put soy grits, water, tomato juice, and Worcestershire sauce in large covered pan and bring to boil. Reduce heat and simmer for 10 minutes. Add soy powder and powdered skim milk, mixing well. Cut up onions, tomatoes, and green pepper and add to mixture. Blend in sea salt, pepper, chili powder, paprika, and oil. Simmer for 15 minutes. Just before serving, break an egg into each steaming bowl. *Makes 4 servings.*

Each serving has
21 grams of complete protein
359 calories

Hot Chili 'n' Bean Thoup

  1½ cups soybeans (frozen in ice tray)
  1 cup water
  1 cup tomato juice
  4 tomatoes
  ⅛ teaspoon Tabasco sauce
  2 onions
  6 cloves garlic
  1 green pepper
  ½ cup soy powder
  ¼ cup wheat germ
  2 tablespoons safflower oil
  2 teaspoons chili powder
  ⅛ teaspoon paprika
  1 bay leaf
  3 whole cloves
  2 teaspoons sea salt
  ⅛ teaspoon cayenne pepper

Drop frozen soybeans in boiling water and simmer in a covered pot for 1 hour. If you like the beans crunchier, simmer only for ½ hour. Add tomato juice. Cut up tomatoes, onions, and pepper and add with Tabasco sauce. Mince the garlic and add. Slowly stir in soy powder and wheat germ until smooth. Add safflower oil, chili powder, paprika, bay leaf, cloves, sea salt, and cayenne pepper. Simmer for another ½ hour.

Makes 4 servings.

Each serving has
33 grams of complete protein
497 calories

Tomato Cheese Thoup

2 heaping tablespoons soy powder
2 heaping tablespoons noninstant powdered skim
  milk
2 teaspoons sea salt
½ teaspoon basil
½ cup water
1 cup tomato juice
2 tablespoons Worcestershire sauce
2 tablespoons safflower oil
4 large ripe tomatoes
2 green peppers, chopped
2 onions, chopped
1 cup Cheddar cheese, grated

Mix soy powder, powdered skim milk, sea salt, and basil in large covered pan. Add water, tomato juice, Worcestershire sauce, and oil and mix till smooth. Cover and bring to a simmer. Cut tomatoes into tiny pieces and add to mixture with green peppers and onions. Cook for 5 minutes, then add grated cheese and stir until it is melted. Simmer for another 10 minutes.

Makes 4 servings.

Each serving has
16 grams of complete protein
322 calories

Borscht Thoup

2 cups water
1 cup yogurt
½ cup skim milk cottage cheese
2 onions, diced

1 teaspoon sea salt
½ teaspoon rosemary
1⅓ teaspoons granulated sugar substitute
3 tablespoons wine vinegar
2 tablespoons safflower oil
6 pitted prunes
2 heaping tablespoons soy powder
2 heaping tablespoons noninstant powdered skim milk
6 large beets, finely diced

Put water, yogurt, cottage cheese, onions, sea salt, rosemary, sugar substitute, vinegar, safflower oil, and prunes in blender and mix for 30 seconds. Pour into a pan and bring to boil. Stir in soy powder and powdered skim milk and mix well. Add beets to mixture. Simmer for 15 minutes. *Makes 4 servings.*

Each serving has
15 grams of complete protein
266 calories

Creamy Onion Thoup

4 tablespoons safflower oil
4 onions, chopped
1 cup water
½ cup soy powder
⅔ cup noninstant powdered skim milk
1 teaspoon sea salt
½ teaspoon pepper
½ teaspoon chervil
2 cups skim milk
½ cup grated Parmesan cheese

Pour oil into large covered pan. Sauté onions lightly. Add 1 cup water. Blend in soy powder, powdered skim milk, salt, pepper, and chervil. Simmer for 15 minutes. Slowly add skim milk and simmer for 5 minutes. Put grated Parmesan cheese atop each bowl. *Makes 4 servings.*

Each serving has
25 grams of complete protein
398 calories

Curried Thoup

2 cups water
4 cubes or packages vegetable bouillon
4 egg yolks
2 tablespoons safflower oil
1 cup yogurt
1 teaspoon sea salt
½ teaspoon paprika
2 teaspoons curry powder
¼ teaspoon ground cloves
½ tart apple
¼ cup soy powder
½ cup noninstant powdered skim milk

Put water, vegetable consommé, egg yolks, safflower oil, yogurt, sea salt, paprika, curry powder, and cloves in blender for 1 minute. Pour into covered pan and simmer for 10 minutes. Cut up apple and add. Slowly stir in soy powder and powdered skim milk until blended well. Serve hot. *Makes 4 servings.*

Each serving has
15 grams of complete protein
250 calories

Minestrone Thoup

1 onion, chopped
4 carrots, diced
4 celery stalks, diced
2 cups water
4 packages vegetable bouillon
½ cup soy grits
2 tomatoes, diced
1 cup chopped cabbage
¼ cup soy powder
¾ cup grated Parmesan cheese
1 tablespoon safflower oil
1 tablespoon olive oil
1 teaspoon basil leaves
1 teaspoon sage leaves
2 tablespoons parsley, chopped
2 garlic cloves, minced

Put onion, carrots, and celery in water in large pot and bring to boil. Add bouillon and blend well. Add soy grits, tomatoes, cabbage, soy powder, cheese, safflower oil, and olive oil, mixing well. Add basil leaves, sage leaves, parsley, and garlic. Simmer in covered pot for 1 hour.   *Makes 4 servings.*

Each serving has
20 grams of complete protein
343 calories

Italian Risotto Thoup

2 tablespoons safflower oil
2 tablespoons olive oil
2 cloves garlic, minced
2 tablespoons parsley, minced
1 cup mushrooms, chopped
1 cup tomatoes
2 cups water
½ cup soy powder
½ cup noninstant powdered skim milk
2 teaspoons sea salt
2 teaspoons pepper
½ cup uncooked brown rice
¾ cup grated Parmesan cheese
½ teaspoon oregano

Heat safflower oil and olive oil in large covered pan and put in garlic, parsley, and mushrooms. Cook 3 minutes. Add tomatoes and water and simmer covered for 20 minutes. Add soy powder and powdered skim milk and blend thoroughly. Add sea salt, pepper, and brown rice. Simmer for 30 minutes. When ready to serve stir in cheese and oregano.   *Makes 4 servings.*

Each serving has
21 grams of complete protein
390 calories

Okra Thoup

2 cups chopped okra
1 onion, chopped
1 stalk celery, minced
2 tablespoons safflower oil

½ cup skim milk cottage cheese
4 tablespoons catsup
4 cubes or packages vegetable bouillon
½ cup soy powder
½ cup soy grits
1 tablespoon chopped basil leaf
1 teaspoon sea salt
½ teaspoon pepper
½ teaspoon saffron powder
2 cups water

Put okra, onion, and celery in large pan with oil and sauté till browned. Add cottage cheese and blend well. Add catsup, bouillon, and soy powder, mixing well. Add soy grits, basil leaf, sea salt, pepper and saffron powder. Add water slowly, blending well. Simmer for 1 hour. *Makes 4 servings.*

Each serving has
20 grams of complete protein
276 calories

Greek Casserole

2 tablespoons safflower oil
2 large onions, finely chopped
2 cloves garlic, finely chopped
¼ cup finely chopped parsley
½ teaspoon finely chopped dill
½ teaspoon rosemary
¼ teaspoon dry mustard
4 large tomatoes, chopped
1 cup frozen soybeans
1 cup water
2 cups crumbled feta cheese

Put oil in skillet and add onions, garlic, parsley, dill, rosemary, and dry mustard. Cook and stir for 3 minutes. Add tomatoes, soybeans, and water. Cover and simmer for 20 minutes. Pour into casserole and top with feta cheese. Cover casserole and bake for 1 hour at 400°.   *Makes 4 servings.*

Each serving has
38 grams of complete protein
647 calories

Old West Casserole

1½ cups soybeans (frozen in ice tray)
1 cup water
1 green pepper, chopped
2 tablespoons safflower oil
1 cup mushrooms, diced
1 teaspoon sea salt
1 teaspoon pepper
1 onion, chopped
2 cups tomato sauce
1 whole tomato, diced
8 ripe olives, chopped
1 tablespoon chili powder
2 heaping tablespoons soy powder

Put frozen soybeans in large pot with water and simmer for ½ hour. Add green pepper, oil, mushrooms, sea salt, pepper, onion, tomato sauce, tomato, olives, chili powder, and soy powder and stir well, blending thoroughly. Simmer for 1 hour.
Makes 4 servings.

Each serving has
29 grams of complete protein
480 calories

Asparagus Cheese Casserole

12 asparagus stalks
1 cup skim milk
2 tablespoons safflower oil
1 cup diced American cheese
½ cup cottage cheese
1 teaspoon sea salt
½ teaspoon paprika
⅛ teaspoon turmeric
½ teaspoon pepper
2 heaping tablespoons soy powder
*2 heaping tablespoons noninstant powdered skim
        milk*
¼ cup wheat germ

Chop asparagus stalks to ½-inch pieces and simmer in skim milk in large covered pan over very low flame until tender. Slowly add oil, cheese, cottage cheese, sea salt, paprika, turmeric, pepper, soy powder, and powdered skim milk, stirring constantly until thickened. Alternate layers of asparagus-cheese mixture with a thin layer of wheat germ, topping it with wheat germ. Bake for 15 minutes in 350° oven.　　　　*Makes 4 servings.*

Each serving has
25 grams of complete protein
337 calories

Cauliflower Casserole

    2 eggs
    4 cups tomatoes, cut up
    3 teaspoons granulated sugar substitute
    2 heaping tablespoons soy powder
    4 teaspoons sea salt
    ¼ teaspoon oregano
    ¼ teaspoon marjoram
    4 onions, chopped
    1 head cauliflower, chopped
    1 cup soy grits
    1 tablespoon safflower oil
    juice of 1 lemon

Beat 2 eggs and mix with tomatoes in casserole. Add sugar substitute, soy powder, salt, oregano, and marjoram. Stir in onions, chopped cauliflower, soy grits, and oil. Sprinkle with lemon, cover and bake in moderate oven (350°) for 1 hour.

Makes 4 servings.

    Each serving has
    24 grams of complete protein
    410 calories

Baked Succotash Brazilian

    2 heaping tablespoons noninstant powdered skim
        milk
    2 heaping tablespoons soy powder
    ½ cup skim milk
    1 tablespoon safflower oil
    ½ cup skim milk cottage cheese
    2 eggs

1 cup soy grits
1 cup whole kernel corn
2 tablespoons Worcestershire sauce
1 onion, chopped
1 green pepper, chopped
1 teaspoon sea salt
⅛ teaspoon cayenne pepper
¼ teaspoon chili powder
¼ teaspoon marjoram

Mix powdered skim milk and soy powder with skim milk, oil, and cottage cheese in blender. Add 2 eggs. Pour into baking dish and mix in soy grits, corn, Worcestershire sauce, onion, green pepper, sea salt, cayenne pepper, chili powder, and marjoram. Stir until completely mixed. Bake at 350° for about 1 hour, or until golden brown on top.   *Makes 4 servings.*

Each serving has
26 grams of complete protein
330 calories

Irish Rarebit

2 eggs
2 tablespoons safflower oil
1 tablespoon Worcestershire sauce
1 teaspoon dry mustard
½ teaspoon sea salt
⅛ teaspoon cayenne pepper
½ cup soy powder
¼ cup noninstant powdered skim milk
1½ cups Irish ale
1 cup grated sharp Cheddar cheese

Mix eggs, oil, Worcestershire sauce, mustard, sea salt, and pepper in large teflon-lined pan over very low flame. Slowly add soy powder and powdered skim milk, mixing thoroughly. Gradually add Irish ale, stirring constantly. Then slowly add grated cheese, stirring until very hot and smooth.

Makes 4 servings.

Each serving has
21 grams of complete protein
351 calories

Mushroom Pilaf

4 tablespoons safflower oil
1 cup wheat pilaf
2½ cups water
½ cup soy grits
4 stalks celery, chopped
2 onions, chopped
1 clove garlic, minced
¼ cup soy powder
4 ripe tomatoes, diced
4 tablespoons Worcestershire sauce
1 teaspoon sea salt
1 teaspoon paprika
½ teaspoon thyme
2 cups chopped mushrooms
½ cup skim milk cottage cheese

Heat oil in large covered pan. Add pilaf and stir for 1 minute. Add water and soy grits and simmer for 15 minutes. Add celery, onions, garlic, soy powder, tomatoes, Worcestershire sauce, sea salt, paprika, thyme, and mushrooms and simmer for

30 minutes. Add cottage cheese and cook an additional 10 minutes, stirring constantly.   *Makes 4 servings.*

Each serving has
17 grams of complete protein
452 calories

Soybeans Orientale

3 cups water
1½ cups soybeans (frozen in ice tray)
2 tablespoons safflower oil
½ teaspoon ginger
½ teaspoon curry powder
¼ teaspoon thyme
½ teaspoon pepper
1 teaspoon sea salt
¼ cup brown rice
2 onions, chopped
1 clove garlic, minced
2 tablespoons soy sauce
1 teaspoon granulated sugar substitute

Put water into large covered pot and bring to boil.
Add frozen soybeans, cover and simmer for 1 hour. Add oil,
ginger, curry powder, thyme, pepper, sea salt, brown rice, onions,
garlic, soy sauce and sugar substitute and simmer for 1 more hour.
Makes 4 servings.

Each serving has
26 grams of complete protein
403 calories

Mexican Rarebit

2 eggs
½ cup diced tomatoes
2 tablespoons safflower oil
1 small chopped green pepper
1½ cups grated Cheddar cheese
1 cup whole kernel corn
½ cup noninstant powdered skim milk
¼ cup wheat germ
½ teaspoon sea salt
1 teaspoon chili powder
½ cup soy powder

In a large covered pot mix eggs, tomatoes, oil, green pepper, cheese, and corn. In a large bowl mix powdered skim milk, wheat germ, sea salt, chili powder, and soy powder. Heat the pot till it simmers, then slowly add dry ingredients. Mix well and simmer for 15 minutes, stirring as it thickens.

Makes 6 servings.

Each serving has
21 grams of complete protein
317 calories

Tomatoes with Cheese

1 cup cottage cheese with chives
½ cup wheat germ
8 fresh tomatoes
1 teaspoon sea salt
½ teaspoon pepper
½ teaspoon oregano
1 cup shredded Cheddar cheese
¼ cup chopped onions

Mix cottage cheese with wheat germ. Cover the bottom of a casserole with mixture. Add a layer of fresh tomatoes, cut in ½″ slices. Sprinkle with sea salt, pepper, and oregano. Top with layer of shredded Cheddar cheese mixed with chopped onion. Bake at 350° for 30 minutes. *Makes 4 servings.*

Each serving has
22 grams of complete protein
295 calories

Argentine Puchero Sin Carne

2 cups water
1½ cups soybeans (frozen in ice tray)
2 cloves garlic, minced
2 onions, chopped
4 tablespoons catsup
1 tablespoon crushed peppercorns
1 teaspoon sea salt
4 stalks celery, chopped
2 turnips, halved
4 carrots, quartered
4 zucchini, halved lengthwise
½ head cabbage in 4 wedges
½ teaspoon basil

Bring water to a boil in a large pot and drop in frozen cubes of soybeans. Add garlic, onions, catsup, peppercorns, sea salt, celery, turnips, carrots, zucchini, cabbage, and basil and cook over very low flame for 1 hour. *Makes 4 servings.*

Each serving has
26 grams of complete protein
413 calories

Stuft Peppers

1 cup soy grits
1½ cups water
1 tablespoon safflower oil
¼ teaspoon sea salt
¼ teaspoon dry mustard
¼ teaspoon pepper
¼ teaspoon nutmeg
1 egg
2 tablespoons diced celery
1 diced onion
1 minced clove garlic
2 heaping tablespoons soy powder
2 tablespoons wheat germ
6 medium green peppers

Put soy grits and water into a pan and add oil, sea salt, mustard, pepper, and nutmeg. Bring to a boil, then simmer until most of the water is absorbed. Beat in the egg and add celery, onion, garlic, soy powder, and wheat germ. Mix well and simmer for 15 minutes with lid on pan. Remove tops and seeds from peppers, then stuff with mixture. Put in oven at 300° for 40 minutes, or until peppers are tender.   *Makes 6 servings.*

Each serving has
16 grams of complete protein
234 calories

Cheesy Stuft Peppers

4 large green peppers
¼ cup wheat germ
1 cup cottage cheese

1 onion, chopped finely
1 tablespoon mayonnaise
1 tablespoon safflower oil
2 eggs
1 teaspoon sea salt
1 teaspoon pepper
½ teaspoon rosemary
½ teaspoon paprika
¾ cup diced American cheese

Remove tops and seeds from peppers. Into a large bowl mix wheat germ, cottage cheese, onion, mayonnaise, oil, and eggs. Blend thoroughly. Add sea salt, pepper, rosemary, paprika, and ½ cup American cheese. Fill peppers with mixture. Place in a casserole and top with remaining crumbled American cheese. Bake in moderate oven (350°) for 45 minutes.

Makes 4 servings.

Each serving has
22 grams of complete protein
309 calories

High-Prote, Low-Cal Spaghetti or Macaroni

1 cup (4 oz.) dry, enriched, low-calorie spaghetti or
    macaroni
1 teaspoon sea salt
2 tablespoons safflower oil
1 cup cottage cheese with chives
2 cloves garlic, finely minced
1 teaspoon sea salt
½ teaspoon pepper

Put spaghetti or macaroni into a large pan of boiling water. Add 1 teaspoon sea salt. Boil at a fast boil until tender (usually about 10 minutes). Pour into a collander (straining dish) and when most of the water is drained off, pour into a large skillet. Add safflower oil, mix well and heat. Add cottage cheese, garlic, sea salt, and pepper, mixing well until very hot and cottage cheese becomes a little stringy. Serve very hot.   *Makes 2 servings.*

Each serving has
20 grams of complete protein
445 calories

Chivey-Cheese Pie

1 cup skim milk
4 tablespoons skim milk cottage cheese
2 eggs
½ cup chopped chives
1 cup chopped onions
2 tablespoons safflower oil
1 teaspoon sea salt
½ teaspoon pepper
½ teaspoon paprika
½ teaspoon dry mustard
1 tablespoon Worcestershire sauce
2 heaping tablespoons soy powder
2 heaping tablespoons noninstant powdered skim
    milk
1½ cups shredded Cheddar cheese
4 tablespoons wheat germ

Put skim milk, cottage cheese, eggs, chives, onions, oil, sea salt, pepper, paprika, mustard, and Worcestershire sauce in blender and mix for 30 seconds. Slowly add soy powder and powdered skim milk and blend for 15 seconds. Pour into glass pie dish and sprinkle Cheddar cheese evenly throughout mixture. Top with wheat germ. Bake at 350° for 30 minutes.

Makes 4 servings.

Each serving has
32 grams of complete protein
475 calories

Peppers Stuft with Mushrooms

2 cups chopped fresh mushrooms
1½ cups tomato sauce
1 teaspoon sea salt
¼ teaspoon pepper
1 teaspoon onion juice
2 tablespoons wheat germ
1 cup cottage cheese with chives
1 tablespoon safflower oil
½ cup soy powder
½ cup noninstant powdered skim milk
6 medium green peppers
½ cup grated Cheddar cheese

Blend mushrooms with 1 cup tomato sauce, sea salt, pepper, onion juice, wheat germ, cottage cheese, oil, soy powder, and powdered skim milk. Remove tops and seeds from peppers. Place peppers in muffin tins and stuff with mushroom mixture. Cover with Cheddar cheese and bake in 350° oven for 30 minutes. Pour remaining ½ cup tomato sauce on top of each stuffed pepper and bake 10 more minutes. *Makes 6 servings.*

Each serving has
19 grams of complete protein
240 calories

Cheese Dumplings

1 cup water
1 tablespoon safflower oil
½ teaspoon sea salt
¼ teaspoon mace
½ teaspoon pepper
¼ teaspoon dry mustard
½ cup whole wheat flour
¼ cup soy powder
¼ cup wheat germ (untoasted)
3 eggs
1 cup grated Parmesan cheese
1 cup Cheesy Sauce (Chapter 7)

Put water, oil, sea salt, mace, pepper, and dry mustard in pan and bring to boil. Slowly add whole wheat flour, soy powder, and wheat germ. Stir for 2 minutes. Beat in 1 egg and continue stirring for 3 minutes. Beat in 2 more eggs and mix thoroughly. Add grated cheese, stirring constantly. Fill another large pan with water and bring to a boil. Drop dough from tablespoon into boiling water. After dumplings rise, let boil for 3 minutes. Take out and place in baking dish and cover with Cheesy Sauce. Bake at 400° for 20 minutes, or until golden brown.

Makes 4 servings.

Each serving has
32 grams of complete protein
455 calories

5

Salad Days (and Nights)

ORIGINAL IDEAS FOR HIGH-PROTE SALADS

Noah Webster says salad days mean a time of youthful inexperience. It's also the best time, and way, to lose weight. If every day for a week a tubby person were to eat a high-protein salad for dinner with a glass of skim milk, within that week several pounds would disappear with no afterpangs of hunger, and a terrific glow of well-being would follow. I've tried it and it works. Even though you may eat a big lunch, usually the most gluttonous stuffing-time of the day is dinner. If you can keep the cals down *there*, you've got it made. To help you do that, you'll find some pretty wild salads here.

The Sunflower Salad makes a meal that's light yet filling. As you crunch your way through it you'll be happy to know that sunflower seeds are absolutely fantastic for your eyes. They're loaded with the B vites which are as necessary as Vitamin A for the eyes. I started eating about half a cup a day, and my eyes really improved. I don't need to wear my shades as often and I can actually see better. So I use the seeds lots of ways. And of course you don't have to worry about pesticides 'cause they come out of their shells untouched by human *anything*! So make a Sunflower Salad—17 grams of prote and 382 cals per serving.

The Farmer's Garden Salad has so many different vegetables you could probably eat it every day and not get bored. It'll give you 20 grams of prote and 398 cals.

For an Italian twist serve the Parmesan Beans Salad on beds of lettuce, with an Italian Cheese Cake (Chapter 8) for dessert. The salad will give you 16 grams of prote with 313 cals, and each slice of cheese cake has 19 grams of prote and 257 cals. The total of the salad and cake is 35 prote grams and 570 cals.

If you're ready for something really different (and your pals and family aren't afraid to try new things), you'll wow 'em with Hot Cole Slaw for 11 grams of prote and only 207 cals. And right next to it put a loaf of Raisin Cheese Bread (Chapter 8) for 12 grams of prote and 285 cals per slice. That'll up the prote to 23 with only 492 cals. It's a great combo!

For all you Popeye fans, there's a Spinach Salad. If you've never tried raw spinach, I think you'll like it. It tastes a lot different from cooked spinach and a lot different from lettuce. Each serving gives you 18 grams of prote and only 329 cals. If you serve it with a bowl full of hot Molasses Puffins (Chapter 8), each puffin will give you 7 grams of prote and a low 165 cals. If you eat just one puffin with the salad, you'll get 25 grams of prote and 494 cals.

They say spice is the variety of life. I learned that from my Uncle Bill, who always has a spice garden growing. He introduced me to the incredible bouquet of fresh spices, so now I have a couple of little pots hanging in my kitchen, and I just reach up for a sprig of fresh thyme or sweet marjoram. And I keep several small pepper mills, one filled with fresh peppercorns, and the others with cardamom seed (great in curries and thoups), celery seeds (for salads and sauerkraut), coriander seed (tastes like sage and lemon peel), and lots more. The flavor of something freshly ground is very different from that of something ground weeks, months, or years before and then bottled.

Here's a list of spices and their uses.

Allspice   Tastes like a combination of cloves, cinnamon, and nutmeg. A multipurpose spice.

Anise   Smells and tastes like licorice. Used in breads, candies, and sweet pickles.

Basil   Tastes a little like cloves. Used in soups, "thoups," and stews, and is perfect mixed with any form of tomato.

Bay leaves   Used in stews, roasts, sauces, fish, meat loaf, meatballs.

Caraway seed   Used with cottage cheese, rye bread, cabbage, fish chowders.

Cardamom seed   Has a pungent flavor. Used in pastries and curries.

Celery seeds   Gives a celery flavor. Used in salads, sauerkraut, soups, "thoups," and in pickling.

Chervil   An aromatic herb like parsley. Used in salads, soups, and "thoups."

Chili powder   Very tangy flavor. Used in all Mexican dishes, cocktail sauce, hamburgers, and meat loaf.

Cinnamon   A distinctive flavor. Used in cakes, pies, puddings, for cinnamon toast, applesauce, baked apple, atop coffee and Sanka.

Cloves	Unbelievably great fragrance. For a sensational room perfumer and to get rid of bad odors, put a teaspoon of cloves in a cup, fill with boiling water, and set out on a table— *quel* smell!! Also used for baked ham, mincemeat, catsup, chili sauce, pies, cookies, cakes.
Coriander seed	Tastes like sage and lemon peel mixed. Used in meat dishes, salads.
Cumin	Slightly bitter, an appetite whetter. Used with meat, bread, pickling.
Curry powder	A highly seasoned East Indian spice. Used with meats, eggs, fish.
Dill	An aromatic herb. Used in seafood, cabbage, pickles, sauces.
Fennel	Tastes a little like anise, which tastes like licorice. Used in pies, cakes, cookies, and even for pickles.
File	Made from leaves of sassafras tree. Used in gumbo dishes and other Creole things.
Ginger	Very spicy and tangy. Used in Chinese dishes, pies, cakes, cookies, relishes, vegetables, meats, fish.
Mace	Made from nutmeg covering, but tastes completely different. Used for gravies and meat stuffings, fish, meats, cakes, and pies.
Marjoram	An all-round spice. Used with vegetables, seafood, poultry, meats, cold cuts.
Mustard	Very tangy and biting. Used for almost every-

thing from vegetables, meats, pickling, sauces, dressings, fish.

Nutmeg	Wonderfully different flavor. Used in pies, cakes, cookies, puddings, vegetables, eggnogs, hot cocoa.
Oregano	Aromatic, not unlike marjoram. Used in most Italian dishes, meats, tomato sauces, salad dressings, soups, and "thoups."
Paprika	Made from sweet red peppers, mild and tangy. Used in Hungarian dishes, salads, cheeses, cottage cheese, sauces, dressings.
Parsley	An aromatic herb like chervil. Used in salads, soups, "thoups," stews, meat loaf, and meatballs.
Pepper (Black)	A distinctive, biting flavor. Used in everything not sweet.
(White)	The same as black pepper except the outer hull and some of the flavor are removed. More appetizing on some foods than black pepper.
(Red)	Known as cayenne pepper. Very hot. Used for extra bite in soups, "thoups," cottage cheese, cheeses, meat, fish, eggs.
Poppy seed	Mild, different flavor. Used in pastries, breads, rolls, cheeses.
Rosemary	Mild and aromatic. Used with vegetables, sauces, poultry, fish, gravies.
Saffron	Tastes like sandalwood smells. Used in Spanish cooking, rice dishes.
Sage	Pungent and aromatic. Used in soups,

	"thoups," fish, stuffings, dumplings, meats, vegetables, stews.
Savory	Used particularly with fish that needs enhancement.
Tarragon	Distinctive fragrance. Used for all hot and cold fish, vegetables, poultry, sauces, vinegars.
Thyme	Slightly tangy. Used with chowders, hamburgers, meat loaf, stuffings, tomato dishes.
Turmeric	Part of the ginger family, but milder. Used for pickles, mustards, vegetables.

For me, experimenting with spices and herbs is the best part and most fun of cooking. Add a touch of this and a pinch of that and flavors spring to life. The plainest dish can become exciting when you add a strange and pungent fragrance. They add mystery to food and especially to salads, so try experimenting with the salads here.

Farmer's Garden Salad

1 cup watercress, in small pieces
1 cup lettuce, in small pieces
1 cup chopped tomato
2 tablespoons safflower oil
8 radishes, chopped
4 celery stalks, chopped
1 cup green pepper, chopped
½ cup red pepper, chopped
4 green olives, chopped
4 black olives, chopped
1 cup raw cauliflower, chopped
1 cup cottage cheese with chives
2 teaspoons sea salt
¼ teaspoon cayenne pepper
1 tablespoon soy sauce
1 tablespoon lemon juice

Into a large bowl mix watercress, lettuce, tomato, safflower oil, radishes, celery, green pepper, red pepper, green olives, black olives, cauliflower, cottage cheese, sea salt, pepper, soy sauce and lemon juice. Toss till everything is well mixed. Serve on large beds of lettuce leaves.   *Makes 2 servings.*

Each serving has
20 grams of complete protein
398 calories

Sunflower Salad

1 cup sunflower seeds
1 cup diced celery
2 ripe tomatoes, diced
1 tart apple, diced
4 prunes, cut up
1 teaspoon granulated sugar substitute
4 tablespoons chives
2 tablespoons catsup
1 heaping tablespoon soy powder
1 heaping tablespoon noninstant powdered skim milk
1 teaspoon sea salt
1 teaspoon pepper
2 cups yogurt
1 cup shredded watercress
1 cup shredded romaine lettuce

In a large bowl mix sunflower seeds, celery, tomatoes, apple, prunes, sugar substitute, chives, catsup, soy powder, powdered skim milk, sea salt, pepper, and yogurt. Blend well. Add watercress and romaine lettuce and mix thoroughly.

Makes 4 servings.

Each serving has
17 grams of complete protein
382 calories

Wheat Pilaf Salad

1 cup wheat pilaf
2 tablespoons safflower oil
1 onion, minced

1 cup parsley, minced
4 tablespoons chives, minced
2 tomatoes, chopped
2 tablespoons mint leaves, minced
2 cups water
4 tablespoons lemon juice
½ cup soy powder
1 cup cottage cheese with chives
8 large leaves of lettuce, romaine, or cabbage
1 teaspoon sea salt
½ teaspoon pepper
½ teaspoon coriander seed

Put wheat pilaf in skillet with oil and sauté with onion, parsley, chives, tomatoes, and mint leaves. Pour mixture into pan of boiling water and simmer for 15 minutes. Add lemon juice, soy powder, and cottage cheese. Stir and mix well. Let cool and spoon mixture onto lettuce, romaine, or cabbage leaves. Add sea salt, pepper, and coriander seed. Roll up and fasten with toothpicks. *Makes 4 servings.*

Each serving has
16 grams of complete protein
312 calories

Red and White Salad

1 cup shredded red cabbage
1 cup shredded white cabbage
1 clove garlic, minced
1 cup chopped endive
1 cup chopped red pepper
1 cup chopped radishes
1½ cups Rosy Yogurt Dressing (Chapter 7)

Into a large bowl mix red cabbage, white cabbage, garlic, endive, red pepper and radishes. Pour Rosy Yogurt Dressing and mix well. *Makes 4 servings.*

Each serving has
6 grams of complete protein
186 calories

Carrot and Avacado Salad

1 cup yogurt
1 cup cottage cheese with chives
½ cup soy powder
2 heaping tablespoons noninstant powdered skim milk
1 tablespoon soy sauce
1 onion, minced
4 carrots, grated
½ teaspoon paprika
⅛ teaspoon cayenne pepper
½ teaspoon sea salt
1 teaspoon lemon juice
1 ripe avocado, chopped
romaine
watercress

Mix yogurt and cottage cheese. Add soy powder, powdered skim milk, soy sauce, onion, carrots, paprika, pepper, sea salt and lemon juice. Stir in avocado pieces. Serve on bed of romaine with watercress garnish. *Makes 4 servings.*

Each serving has
16 grams of complete protein
262 calories

Watercress Salad

¼ cup noninstant powdered skim milk
½ cup cottage cheese with chives
2 tomatoes, cut up
2 stalks celery, chopped
1 garlic clove, minced
1 cup ripe olives, minced
4 hard cooked eggs, sliced
2 tablespoons mayonnaise
10 radishes, chopped
1 onion, finely chopped
1 teaspoon sea salt
1 teaspoon pepper
½ teaspoon rosemary
1 bunch watercress, chopped
lettuce leaves

Mix powdered skim milk with cottage cheese. Add tomatoes, celery, garlic, olives, eggs, mayonnaise, radishes, onion, sea salt, pepper, and rosemary. Blend well. Put chopped watercress in a large bowl and add mixture. Toss till well mixed. Serve on lettuce leaves. *Makes 4 servings.*

Each serving has
15 grams of complete protein
282 calories

Seed 'n' Sprout Salad

2 cups bean sprouts
¼ head lettuce, shredded
1 cup watercress, chopped
2 cups sunflower seeds
½ cup sesame seeds
½ cup parsley, chopped
2 stalks celery, chopped
1 small onion, finely chopped
1 cup yogurt
2 tablespoons mayonnaise
½ teaspoon sea salt
½ teaspoon coriander seed
¼ teaspoon paprika

Put bean sprouts, lettuce, watercress, sunflower seeds, sesame seeds, parsley, celery, and onion in large bowl. In a separate dish blend yogurt, mayonnaise, sea salt, coriander seed, and paprika and pour over salad, mixing well. *Makes 4 servings.*

Each serving has
24 grams of complete protein
626 calories

Cold Stuft Tomatoes

4 large ripe tomatoes
1 cup skim milk cottage cheese
½ cup yogurt
2 tablespoons safflower oil
2 heaping tablespoons soy powder
2 heaping tablespoons noninstant powdered skim
    milk

1 tablespoon chopped chives
2 tablespoons minced onion
1 teaspoon sea salt
½ teaspoon paprika
½ teaspoon dry mustard
½ teaspoon tarragon
½ cup Hard Egg Dressing (Chapter 7)

Cut off stem ends and scoop out insides of tomatoes. Mix pulp with cottage cheese, yogurt, safflower oil, soy powder, powdered skim milk, chives, onion, sea salt, paprika, mustard, and tarragon. Stuff tomatoes with mixture and top with Hard Egg Dressing. *Makes 4 servings.*

Each serving has
22 grams of complete protein
351 calories

Parmesan Beans Salad

2 cups string beans, chopped
¼ cup water
1 onion, chopped
4 tablespoons safflower oil
4 tablespoons cider vinegar
½ teaspoon sea salt
¼ teaspoon ginger
¼ teaspoon paprika
2 heaping tablespoons soy powder
2 heaping tablespoons noninstant powdered skim
    milk
¾ cup grated Parmesan cheese
lettuce leaves
tomato wedges

Put beans in water, bring to a boil, and simmer. Add onion, safflower oil, vinegar, sea salt, ginger, paprika, soy powder, powdered skim milk, and Parmesan cheese. Cover and cook over very low flame for 20 minutes. Chill and serve on lettuce leaves. Garnish with tomato wedges. *Makes 4 servings.*

Each serving has
16 grams of complete protein
313 calories

Oriental Delight

1½ cups yogurt
6 tablespoons mayonnaise
⅛ teaspoon sea salt
1 cup bean sprouts
¼ cup chopped kumquats
1⅓ teaspoons granulated sugar substitute
½ cup chopped pineapple (no sugar)
¼ cup soy powder
½ cup noninstant powdered skim milk
⅔ cup chopped almonds
1 tablespoon chopped fresh ginger
lettuce leaves
watercress

Mix yogurt, mayonnaise, sea salt, bean sprouts, kumquats, sugar substitute, pineapple, soy powder, powdered skim milk, almonds, and ginger. Blend everything well. Pile onto lettuce leaves with watercress garnish. *Makes 4 servings.*

Each serving has
17 grams of complete protein
467 calories

Soybean Salad

1 heaping tablespoon noninstant powdered skim
   milk
1 heaping tablespoon soy powder
½ cup yogurt
4 tablespoons mayonnaise
4 tablespoons pickle relish
2 tablespoons catsup
½ teaspoon sea salt
½ teaspoon pepper
¼ teaspoon coriander seed
2 stalks celery, chopped
1 green pepper, chopped
1 red pepper, chopped
2 hard cooked eggs, chopped
3 cups cooked soybeans (1 cup raw becomes 3 cups
   cooked)
lettuce leaves

Mix powdered skim milk and soy powder with yogurt, mayonnaise, pickle relish, catsup, sea salt, pepper, and coriander seed. Mix well. Add celery, green pepper, red pepper, eggs, and soybeans. Toss till well blended. Serve on lettuce leaves.

Makes 4 servings.

Each serving has
24 grams of complete protein
432 calories

Hot Cole Slaw

    4 egg yolks
    1 teaspoon granulated sugar substitute
    ½ teaspoon sea salt
    ½ teaspoon paprika
    ½ teaspoon celery seed
    ½ tablespoon caraway seeds
    ½ cup apple cider vinegar
    2 tablespoons safflower oil
    2 heaping tablespoons soy powder
    2 heaping tablespoons noninstant powdered skim
        milk
    ½ cup yogurt
    1 head of cabbage, shredded (4 cups)

Mix egg yolks, sugar substitute, sea salt, paprika, celery seed, caraway seeds, vinegar, safflower oil, soy powder, and powdered skim milk in a pan. Bring almost to a boil and add yogurt, stirring constantly. Pour mixture over shredded cabbage and mix thoroughly. *Makes 4 servings.*

    Each serving has
    11 grams of complete protein
    207 calories

Chili Salad

    1 cup skim milk cottage cheese
    1 cup Mexican Chili Sauce (Chapter 7)
    6 tablespoons mayonnaise
    ½ teaspoon sea salt
    ½ teaspoon pepper
    1 cup yogurt

1 large chopped green pepper
¼ cup soy powder
½ cup noninstant powdered skim milk
2 tablespoons safflower oil
½ cup chopped radishes
4 hard cooked eggs
romaine

Mix cottage cheese, chili sauce, mayonnaise, sea salt, pepper, yogurt, green pepper, soy powder, powdered skim milk, safflower oil, and radishes and blend well. Serve on romaine leaves and put 4 egg quarters around each plate.

Makes 4 servings.

Each serving has
25 grams of complete protein
524 calories

Spinach Salad

¼ cup cider vinegar
¼ cup safflower oil
¼ cup water
½ cup cottage cheese with chives
1 onion, chopped
2 heaping tablespoons soy powder
2 heaping tablespoons noninstant powdered skim milk
1 teaspoon granulated sugar substitute
1 teaspoon sea salt
½ teaspoon tarragon
½ teaspoon pepper
4 hard cooked eggs
1 large bunch chopped raw spinach (about 4 cups)

Put vinegar, oil, water, cottage cheese, onion, soy powder, powdered skim milk, sugar substitute, sea salt, tarragon, and pepper in blender and blend for 30 seconds. Chop hard cooked eggs into small pieces and put in blender for 5 seconds. Pour over spinach in large bowl, mixing well. *Makes 4 servings.*

Each serving has
18 grams of complete protein
329 calories

Baked Salad

¼ cup soy powder
¼ cup noninstant powdered skim milk
1 teaspoon sea salt
½ teaspoon pepper
½ teaspoon basil
⅛ teaspoon cayenne pepper
1 cup cottage cheese with chives
4 stalks celery, finely chopped
2 cups watercress, chopped
1 green pepper, chopped
8 radishes, chopped
1 cucumber, peeled and chopped finely
2 tomatoes, diced
1 clove garlic, minced
2 onions, chopped
2 tablespoons safflower oil
2 eggs
2 tablespoons soy sauce

Into a large bowl mix soy powder, powdered skim milk, sea salt, pepper, basil, cayenne pepper, and cottage cheese. Blend thoroughly. Add celery, watercress, green pepper, radishes, cucumber, tomatoes, garlic, onions, and safflower oil. Beat eggs in separate bowl with soy sauce, then blend into mixture. Pour into large casserole and bake for 1 hour at 350°f. *Makes 4 servings.*

Each serving has
19 grams of complete protein
276 calories

6

Vive le Vegetable

HOW TO MAKE INCOMPLETE
VEGETABLE PROTEIN COMPLETE

LOTS OF PEOPLE think if you don't eat meat you're a vegetarian —but that's not necessarily true. A vegetarian eats *only* vegetables. If you eat eggs, cheese, and other proteins from animal sources you're not a vegetarian, just a no-meat eater.

Some people also think that if you don't eat meat you'll be pale and weak, but just look at the animals. What's the fastest animal in the world? The thoroughbred race horse, a vegetarian. What's the toughest animal of all? The elephant, that's what. And don't mess with a rhino either. They're both vegetarians. Obviously you can be rough and tough and fast and strong and not eat meat. The predators (lions, tigers, alligators, snakes, wolves, man) all eat flesh. Even hawks eat meat, but doves don't! Think about it when

92

you think about love and peace. That's love and peace for every living thing. And remember, the protein from eggs, milk, cheese, and other nonmeat products have more of the essential amino acids than the protein from meat.

For openers in the vegetable department, try one of the "smashers," like Smashed Zucchini. It's creamy with a never-before kind of flavor. One serving has 4 protein grams and only 83 calories.

You'll love the Armenian Green Beans. They have a distinctive Middle East flavor that's different. And you'll get 4 grams of prote and 148 cals.

One serving of Creamy Spinach will give you 5 grams of prote with 125 cals. You cook it in skim milk, so all the vites and iron are left in.

Stuft Tomatoes are terrific and easy to make. Each one provides 8 grams of prote and 183 calories. Stuft Squash takes a while to bake, but it's easy to make too. Each serving has 17 grams of prote and only 168 calories.

A really exotic dish is Mushrooms in Yogurt. It's highly seasoned and may be the most different vegetable dish you've ever tasted. Each serving has 6 grams of prote and 140 cals.

Beansprouts, my all-time favorite vegetable, are loaded with enzymes and Vitamin C and all the B vites and are absolutely fantastic for you. When I crunched into my first bean sprout as a kid, I was hooked. The problem was I could only get 'em at Chinese restaurants, so I didn't eat 'em very often.

Then I saw an ad for a sprouter and sent away for one. It cost only a few dollars and gave me my own little vitamin farm. Now it sits in my kitchen—a simple contraption with three sprouting beds, a draining basin for daily rewatering, and no possibility of a mistake. You sprinkle seeds in one sprouting bed each day and three days later you harvest your first crop. I use mung beans (bought in Chinatown) but soy, alfalfa, sesame, wheat, and others will also work. (Don't use potato sprouts because they're poisonous.)

My favorite way of fixing the sprouts is to put a handful in a pan and sprinkle with soy sauce. Heat but don't cook (some of their value is destroyed in cooking). They stay crunchy this way and are really delicious.

Now you can start vegetablizing and get perfect, complete prote and lots of vitamins too.

Armenian Green Beans

1 heaping tablespoon soy powder
1 heaping tablespoon noninstant powdered skim
   milk
1 teaspoon granulated sugar substitute
2 teaspoons sea salt
½ teaspoon oregano
1 teaspoon pepper
⅛ teaspoon ginger
¼ cup water
¼ cup tomato juice
2 tablespoons safflower oil
2 large ripe tomatoes, diced
2 onions, diced
2 cups green beans, chopped
⅛ teaspoon Tabasco sauce

Mix soy powder, powdered skim milk, sugar substitute, sea salt, oregano, pepper, and ginger in a large covered pan. Add water, tomato juice, and oil and mix thoroughly. Add tomatoes, onions, beans, and Tabasco sauce, bring to a boil, and simmer for 15 minutes, stirring frequently.   *Makes 4 servings.*

Each serving has
4 grams of complete protein
148 calories

Creamy Spinach

2 tablespoons safflower oil
1 heaping tablespoon soy powder
1 heaping tablespoon noninstant powdered skim
    milk
¾ cup skim milk
2 cups finely chopped spinach
½ teaspoon sea salt
¼ teaspoon pepper
⅛ teaspoon nutmeg
⅛ teaspoon ginger

Blend oil, soy powder, and powdered skim milk in covered saucepan. Gradually add milk, keeping mixture smooth. Cook over low heat, stirring constantly until mixture thickens. Add spinach, sea salt, pepper, nutmeg, and ginger, blending thoroughly. Simmer for 5 minutes. *Makes 4 servings.*

Each serving has
5 grams of complete protein
125 calories

Smashed Peas

1½ cups shelled peas
4 tablespoons water
1 heaping tablespoon soy powder
2 heaping tablespoons noninstant powdered skim
    milk
1 tablespoon safflower oil
2 tablespoons skim milk
¼ teaspoon marjoram
½ teaspoon granulated sugar substitute

Simmer peas in water in covered pan over very low flame for 15 minutes. Mash and add soy powder, powdered skim milk, oil, skim milk, marjoram, and sugar substitute. Mix well and simmer 5 minutes.   *Makes 4 servings.*

Each serving has
6 grams of complete protein
126 calories

Creamy Carrots

1 heaping tablespoon soy powder
2 heaping tablespoons noninstant powdered skim
    milk
½ cup water
1 tablespoon safflower oil
½ teaspoon granulated sugar substitute
½ cup yogurt
1 teaspoon sea salt
1 teaspoon paprika
1 tablespoon Worcestershire sauce
4 large carrots, sliced
½ teaspoon chervil

Mix soy powder, powdered skim milk, and water in covered saucepan. Add oil, sugar substitute, yogurt, sea salt, paprika, Worcestershire sauce and mix well. Add carrots and chervil and simmer for 30 minutes, stirring frequently.

Makes 4 servings.

Each serving has
6 grams of complete protein
122 calories

Creamy Cabbage

> 3 heaping tablespoons noninstant powdered skim
>   milk
> 1½ cups water
> 4 cups shredded cabbage
> 1 heaping tablespoon soy powder
> 1 teaspoon sea salt
> ½ teaspoon pepper
> 1 tablespoon safflower oil
> ½ cup yogurt
> ½ cup sliced pimiento olives
> 1 teaspoon paprika
> 1 teaspoon caraway seeds

Mix powdered skim milk and water in covered pan. Add cabbage and bring to boil, then simmer over very low flame for about 15 minutes or until tender. In a separate bowl mix soy powder, sea salt, pepper, oil, and yogurt and blend until smooth. Stir into cabbage mixture and simmer until thickened. Add olives, paprika, and caraway seeds and simmer about 5 minutes, stirring constantly.   *Makes 4 servings.*

> Each serving has
> 8 grams of complete protein
> 156 calories

Creamy Broccoli

> 1 heaping tablespoon soy powder
> 1 heaping tablespoon noninstant powdered skim
>   milk
> 4 tablespoons catsup
> ¼ teaspoon tarragon

2 teaspoons safflower oil
¼ cup water
½ teaspoon sea salt
2 cloves garlic, minced
4 tablespoons chopped onion
2 cups chopped broccoli
½ teaspoon pepper

Mix soy powder, powdered skim milk, catsup, tarragon, oil, water, sea salt, garlic, and onion in large covered pan and bring to boil. Add broccoli and pepper and simmer for 20 minutes. *Makes 4 servings.*

Each serving has
4 grams of complete protein
166 calories

Sweet 'n' Sour Red Cabbage

4 cups chopped red cabbage
2 sour apples, finely diced
2 tablespoons safflower oil
⅛ cup water
1 heaping tablespoon soy powder
1 heaping tablespoon noninstant powdered skim
   milk
1 teaspoon granulated sugar substitute
2 tablespoons apple cider vinegar
¼ teaspoon sea salt
⅛ teaspoon celery seeds
¼ teaspoon paprika

Put cabbage, apples, oil, and water in covered skillet, bring to boil and simmer 15 minutes. Add soy powder, pow-

dered skim milk, sugar substitute, and vinegar. Stir well and add
sea salt, celery seeds and paprika. Simmer 5 minutes more.

Makes 4 servings.

Each serving has
4 grams of complete protein
159 calories

Zucchini Orientale

1 heaping tablespoon noninstant powdered skim
  milk
1 heaping tablespoon soy powder
1 cup tomato juice
4 large zucchini, diced
1 cup tomatoes, diced
1 teaspoon sea salt
½ teaspoon pepper
1 tablespoon safflower oil
2 tablespoons Worcestershire sauce
½ cup sesame seeds
1 clove garlic, minced

Mix powdered skim milk, soy powder, and tomato
juice. Add zucchini, tomatoes, sea salt, pepper, oil, Worcestershire sauce, sesame seeds, and garlic and bring to a boil. Turn to
very low flame and simmer for 15 minutes, or until tender.

Makes 4 servings.

Each serving has
7 grams of complete protein
229 calories

Smashed Spanish Carrots

    4 large carrots, diced
    4 tablespoons water
    ½ teaspoon granulated sugar substitute
    1 teaspoon saffron
    ½ teaspoon sea salt
    ½ teaspoon pepper
    1 tablespoon Worcestershire sauce
    1 teaspoon honey
    1 tablespoon safflower oil
    4 tablespoons skim milk
    1 heaping tablespoon soy powder
    2 heaping tablespoons noninstant powdered skim
       milk

Simmer carrots in water in covered pan over very low flame for 15 minutes, or until soft. Mash with fork and add sugar substitute, saffron, sea salt, pepper, Worcestershire sauce, honey, oil, skim milk, soy powder, and powdered skim milk. Mix well and simmer 5 minutes. *Makes 4 servings.*

    Each serving has
    6 grams of complete protein
    128 calories

Orangy Beets

1 teaspoon granulated sugar substitute
⅛ cup water
2 tablespoons safflower oil
⅛ cup orange juice
¼ cup vinegar
½ teaspoon sea salt
1 heaping tablespoon noninstant powdered skim milk
1 heaping tablespoon soy powder
½ teaspoon paprika
4 large cooked beets, diced
2 tablespoons grated orange peel

Blend sugar substitute, water, safflower oil, orange juice, vinegar, sea salt, powdered skim milk, soy powder, and paprika. Bring to boil, stirring constantly. Add beets and orange peel. Simmer for 15 minutes. *Makes 4 servings.*

Each serving has
5 grams of complete protein
150 calories

Mushrooms in Yogurt

2 tablespoons safflower oil
2 tablespoons water
2 cups diced mushrooms
1 cup yogurt
1 heaping tablespoon soy powder
1 heaping tablespoon noninstant powdered skim milk
1 teaspoon sea salt

½ teaspoon paprika
¼ teaspoon nutmeg
⅛ teaspoon Tabasco
1 teaspoon Worcestershire sauce

Heat oil and water in large covered skillet. Add mushrooms and simmer for 10 minutes. Add yogurt, soy powder, powdered skim milk, sea salt, paprika, nutmeg, Tabasco, Worcestershire sauce, and simmer 3 more minutes. *Makes 4 servings.*

Each serving has
6 grams of complete protein
140 calories

Smashed Zucchini

4 large zucchini, diced
4 tablespoons water
1 tablespoon safflower oil
½ teaspoon sea salt
½ teaspoon pepper
⅛ teaspoon marjoram
1 heaping tablespoon soy powder
1 heaping tablespoon noninstant powdered skim milk

Simmer zucchini in water in covered pan 10 minutes. Mash zucchini in pan and add oil, sea salt, pepper, marjoram, soy powder, and powdered skim milk, mixing well over very low flame. Simmer 3 minutes. *Makes 4 servings.*

Each serving has
4 grams of complete protein
83 calories

Syrian Smashed Squash

1 large yellow squash
1 teaspoon granulated sugar substitute
½ teaspoon sea salt
⅛ teaspoon cinnamon
⅛ teaspoon ginger
⅛ teaspoon pepper
2 tablespoons safflower oil
2 egg yolks
1 heaping tablespoon soy powder
2 heaping tablespoons noninstant powdered skim
    milk

Bake squash for 1 hour at 325°f. Cut open and spoon out all golden interior. Mash in a pan and add sugar substitute, sea salt, cinnamon, ginger, pepper, safflower oil, egg yolks, soy powder, powdered skim milk and mix well. Serve hot or cold.

Makes 4 servings.

Each serving has
7 grams of complete protein
154 calories

Smashed Turnips

4 medium turnips, diced
2 tablespoons water
2 tablespoons safflower oil
2 tablespoons chives, chopped
½ teaspoon sea salt
½ teaspoon pepper
1 heaping tablespoon soy powder
2 heaping tablespoons noninstant powdered skim
    milk

¼ cup skim milk
⅛ teaspoon rosemary

Cook turnips in water in covered pan over very low flame for 15 minutes, or until soft. Mash with fork and add oil, chives, sea salt, pepper, soy powder, powdered skim milk, skim milk, and rosemary. Mix well and simmer 5 minutes.

Makes 4 servings.

Each serving has
7 grams of complete protein
123 calories

Stuft Hubbard Squash

1 hubbard squash
2 tablespoons safflower oil
1 onion, minced
2 tablespoons Worcestershire sauce
1 cup skim milk cottage cheese
1 teaspoon sea salt
½ teaspoon pepper
1 heaping tablespoon soy powder
2 heaping tablespoons noninstant powdered skim milk

Split squash and bake 1½ hours at 300°f. Remove squash from shell and mash with oil, onion, Worcestershire sauce, cottage cheese, sea salt, pepper, soy powder and powdered skim milk. Refill squash and bake 30 minutes at 350°f.

Makes 4 servings.

Each serving has
17 grams of complete protein
168 calories

Stuft Zucchini

4 large zucchini
2 eggs
½ onion, minced
2 tablespoons parsley, minced
½ teaspoon sea salt
½ teaspoon pepper
½ teaspoon oregano
2 heaping tablespoons noninstant powdered skim milk
1 heaping tablespoon soy powder
½ cup wheat germ
2 tablespoons safflower oil
¾ cup grated Parmesan cheese

Cut zucchini in half lengthwise. Remove pulp with spoon and combine with eggs, onion, parsley, sea salt, pepper, oregano, powdered skim milk, soy powder, wheat germ, 1 tablespoon oil, and half the Parmesan cheese. Mix well and fill zucchini shells. Sprinkle with remaining oil, then sprinkle with remaining cheese. Bake at 350° for 30 minutes.   *Makes 4 servings.*

Each serving has
21 grams of complete protein
318 calories

Stuft Tomatoes

4 large tomatoes
3 tablespoons wheat germ
3 tablespoons onion, minced
½ clove garlic, minced

1 heaping tablespoon soy powder
2 heaping tablespoons soy grits
¼ teaspoon oregano
¼ teaspoon basil
2 tablespoons safflower oil
1 teaspoon sea salt
½ teaspoon pepper

Cut off slice from the stem end of tomatoes and spoon out interior. Put the pulp in a large bowl and add wheat germ, onion, garlic, soy powder, soy grits, oregano, basil, oil, sea salt, and pepper, mixing well. Stuff the tomatoes with this mixture, place in casserole and bake at 350° for 30 minutes.

Makes 4 servings.

Each serving has
8 grams of complete protein
183 calories

Italian Stuft Eggplant

1 eggplant
1 tablespoon safflower oil
1 tablespoon olive oil
1 onion, chopped finely
¼ cup wheat germ
2 heaping tablespoons noninstant powdered skim
    milk
1 heaping tablespoon soy powder
1 egg
1 teaspoon sea salt
1 teaspoon pepper
1 teaspoon oregano
¾ cup grated Parmesan cheese

Bake eggplant 1 hour at 350°. Let it cool and cut in half lengthwise. Scrape out inside and mash with safflower oil, olive oil, onion, wheat germ, powdered skim milk, soy powder, egg, sea salt, pepper, oregano, and half of Parmesan cheese. Mix very well and refill shells. Sprinkle with remaining half of cheese and bake at 350° for 45 minutes. *Makes 4 servings.*

Each serving has
18 grams of complete protein
282 calories

7

Saucy Sauces and Dressy Dressings

HOW TO TURN NOTHING-DISHES INTO HIGH-PROTE DELIGHTS

ONE OF THE HIPPEST THINGS in cooking is to be aware of sauces. You can take a leftover something from last night or a leftover *anything* frozen from last month, and create a whole new dish by using a sensational sauce. Pour it over or mix it into or bake it with whatever you have and everyone will think you've slaved for hours creating a special dish. Don't ever tell that it took only minutes to prepare, or you'll ruin it for the rest of us!

You can make plain old scrambled eggs and pour Hot Mustard Sauce over 'em. They taste so great you'll probably have to go scramble up some more. Each serving of sauce has 4 extra grams of complete protein and only 96 calories. Add that to the prote and cals of 3 eggs and you get 22 grams of prote and 321 cals.

On the other hand, if you pour Orange Marmalade Sauce over poached eggs, you've got a whole other thing going—tart and sweet and tangy with 2 grams of perfect prote per tablespoon and only 39 cals to add to the eggs. Altogether you get 20 grams of protein and 264 calories.

An omelet is easy to whip up in a large skillet. Before folding it over, pour some Mexican Chili Sauce on the top, then fold it and pour some more on. You'll have a great South of the Border dish. Each half cup serving of sauce has 12 grams of prote and 192 cals, and when you add that to the prote and cals of the omelette, you've got 30 grams of prote and only 417 cals. Then just put the rest of the Chili Sauce in a covered jar in the fridge and it'll keep for over a week. You can also freeze it.

A grilled cheese sandwich (only on whole grain bread, natch!) covered with Hot Onion Sauce is hard to beat, and it makes a really nutritious meal. A quarter cup of sauce gives you 8 grams of prote and 100 cals.

Got a sweet tooth you want to fool? Put a topping of Rum Sauce over anything—cakes, puddings, even pancakes (you can call the pancakes Rum Crepes, and do they ever impress!) to make a superdessert. One quarter cup serving of sauce boosts the prote by 8 grams and gives only 113 cals.

Each and every sauce will do just that—really boost the protein deliciously, and they're all so easy to make.

The same with the salad dressings. You can take some lettuce or romaine which could just be an ordinary salad, and by adding a high-prote dressing, you can convert it to a real nutrition-upper.

The Cottage Salad Dressing will turn a large bowl of greens into a meal. A half cup of dressing provides 11 grams of prote and 196 cals. Add a glass of skim milk and you'll have 20 grams of perfect prote.

Another delish topping for a salad is the Raisin Yogurt Dressing. It's a snap to make in your blender—takes all of 30 seconds to mix—and you'll have a really yummy-sweet, good-to-eat, tasty treat. Pour a half cup over your greens and you'll have 11 protein grams and 242 cals.

And nobody says dressings *have* to be used only on salads. Try them on plain vegetables too. The same for the sauces—go wild and experiment. That's what makes cooking really fun!

Rum Sauce

4 eggs
1⅓ teaspoons granulated sugar substitute
2 tablespoons honey
½ cup yogurt
¼ teaspoon sea salt
½ cup soy powder
2 heaping tablespoons noninstant powdered skim
    milk
1 tablespoon safflower oil
1 teaspoon rum flavor

Separate eggs. Put egg yolks in pan and beat with rotary beater till thickened. Add sugar substitute, honey, yogurt, sea salt, soy powder, and powdered skim milk. Blend thoroughly and place over very low flame. Heat till mixture thickens more, about 3 minutes. Add oil and rum flavor. Beat egg whites till stiff and fold into sauce. Cook another 5 minutes, stirring constantly. Serve hot or cold. *Makes 2 cups.*

Each cup has
32 grams of complete protein
452 calories

Maple Molasses Syrup

1¼ cups water
1 teaspoon maple flavor
2 tablespoons blackstrap molasses
2 tablespoons honey
¼ teaspoon sea salt
1 teaspoon granulated sugar substitute
2 heaping tablespoons soy powder

Put water, maple flavor, molasses, and honey in blender and add sea salt, sugar substitute, and soy powder. Blend for 1 minute. *Makes 1 ½ cups.*

Each ½ cup has
5 grams of complete protein
113 calories

Almond Sauce

> *1 cup skim milk*
> *1 cup yogurt*
> *1 tablespoon safflower oil*
> *½ cup soy powder*
> *½ cup noninstant powdered skim milk*
> *⅔ cup almonds, chopped*
> *2 tablespoons chopped onion*
> *2 packages vegetable bouillon*
> *2 tablespoons chopped chives*
> *⅛ teaspoon mace*
> *⅛ teaspoon dry mustard*
> *½ teaspoon sea salt*
> *½ teaspoon paprika*

Put skim milk, yogurt, and safflower oil in blender and add soy powder, powdered skim milk, almonds, onion, bouillon, chives, mace, mustard, sea salt, and paprika and blend for 45 seconds. Pour into saucepan and simmer for 10 minutes, stirring constantly. Serve hot or cold. *Makes 2 cups.*

Each tablespoon has
3 grams of complete protein
44 calories

Lemony Sauce

4 heaping tablespoons soy powder
⅛ teaspoon sea salt
1 teaspoon grated lemon rind
⅛ teaspoon nutmeg
1½ teaspoons granulated sugar substitute
1 teaspoon coriander seed
1 cup water
2 egg yolks
1 tablespoon safflower oil
2 tablespoons lemon juice

Put soy powder, sea salt, lemon rind, nutmeg, sugar substitute, and coriander seed in pan. Slowly add water over very low flame. Beat egg yolks and slowly add with oil and lemon juice, stirring constantly. Cook for 5 minutes. Serve hot or cold.

Makes 1 ¼ cups.

Each tablespoon has
2 grams of complete protein
30 calories

White Sauce

1 tablespoon safflower oil
2 heaping tablespoons soy powder
3 heaping tablespoons noninstant powdered skim
    milk
1 cup skim milk
½ teaspoon sea salt
¼ teaspoon pepper
⅛ teaspoon rosemary

Heat oil in saucepan and blend in soy powder. Mix powdered skim milk with skim milk till smooth and gradually stir into pan. Simmer, stirring constantly till thickened. Season with sea salt, pepper, and rosemary. Serve hot or cold.

Makes 1 ¼ cups.

Each tablespoon has
3 grams of complete protein
34 calories

Orange Marmalade Sauce

2 heaping tablespoons soy powder
2 heaping tablespoons noninstant powdered skim
    milk
1⅓ teaspoons granulated sugar substitute
⅛ teaspoon sea salt
½ cup water
1 tablespoon safflower oil
4 tablespoons grated orange rind
½ cup orange juice
2 egg yolks
1 tablespoon honey

In a saucepan mix soy powder, powdered skim milk sugar substitute, and sea salt. Then slowly add water over a very low flame, stirring constantly. Add oil and orange rind, blending thoroughly. Add orange juice, beat in egg yolks, add honey, and continue stirring till thickened. Serve hot or cold.

Makes 1 ¼ cups.

Each tablespoon has
2 grams of complete protein
39 calories

Creamy Cream Sauce

1 cup skim milk
1 tablespoon safflower oil
2 tablespoons chopped onion
2 tablespoons parsley, chopped
1 heaping tablespoon soy powder
2 heaping tablespoons noninstant powdered skim
    milk
¼ teaspoon sea salt
¼ teaspoon paprika
⅛ teaspoon pepper

Put skim milk, safflower oil, onion, and parsley in blender and mix for 10 seconds. Add soy powder, powdered skim milk, sea salt, paprika, and pepper and blend another 30 seconds. Pour into pan and cook over medium flame, stirring constantly until sauce becomes creamy. *Makes 1 cup.*

Each tablespoon has
2 grams of complete protein
27 calories

Béarnaise Sauce

6 egg yolks
2 tablespoons safflower oil
¼ cup hot water
½ teaspoon sea salt
⅛ teaspoon cayenne pepper
2 heaping tablespoons noninstant powdered skim
    milk
1 tablespoon lemon juice

Beat egg yolks until thick and lemon colored. Stir in oil and water. Cook in double boiler and stir till thickened. Remove and beat in sea salt, pepper, powdered skim milk, and lemon juice. Serve hot or cold. *Makes 1 ½ cups.*

Each tablespoon has
2 grams of complete protein
31 calories

Hollandaise Sauce

3 egg yolks
2 tablespoons lemon juice
4 tablespoons safflower oil
½ cup hot water
2 tablespoons chopped parsley
2 tablespoons chopped onion
½ teaspoon sea salt
⅛ teaspoon pepper
1 heaping tablespoon soy powder
2 heaping tablespoons noninstant powdered skim milk

Put egg yolks, lemon juice, oil, and water in blender and mix for 10 seconds. Add parsley, onion, sea salt, pepper, soy powder and powdered skim milk and blend for 45 seconds. Pour into pan and cook over very low flame, stirring constantly till sauce thickens. Serve hot or cold. *Makes 1 cup.*

Each tablespoon has
2 grams of complete protein
56 calories

Cheesy Sauce

3 tablespoons safflower oil
4 heaping tablespoons soy powder
½ teaspoon sea salt
¼ teaspoon pepper
¼ teaspoon paprika
6 drops Tabasco sauce
½ cup noninstant powdered skim milk
2 cups skim milk
1 cup grated Cheddar cheese

Heat oil in pan, stir in soy powder and add seasonings. Add powdered skim milk to skim milk and mix until smooth. Add to mixture in pan and simmer until partially thickened, stirring constantly. Add cheese and continue cooking and stirring until cheese is melted. *Makes 3 cups.*

Each cup has
36 grams of complete protein
518 calories

Hot Mustard Sauce

3 tablespoons hot English mustard
1⅓ teaspoons granulated sugar substitute
1 cup cider vinegar
2 heaping tablespoons soy powder
1 egg
1 tablespoon safflower oil
1 teaspoon sea salt
1 teaspoon white pepper
⅛ teaspoon cayenne pepper

Combine mustard, sugar substitute, vinegar, and soy powder. Cook over very low flame for 3 minutes. Beat egg and add to mixture. Continue cooking till thickened, stirring constantly. Stir in oil, sea salt, pepper, and cayenne pepper and remove from heat. Serve hot or cold.   *Makes 1 ¼ cups.*

Each tablespoon has
1 gram of complete protein
24 calories

Curry Sauce

1 onion, chopped finely
2 apples, diced finely
2 tablespoons safflower oil
¼ teaspoon ground cloves
1 tablespoon curry powder
4 heaping tablespoons noninstant powdered skim milk
2 heaping tablespoons soy powder
3 teaspoons lemon juice
½ cup yogurt
2 tablespoons Worcestershire sauce

Combine onion, apples, safflower oil, cloves, curry powder, powdered skim milk, and soy powder in saucepan. Stir in lemon juice, yogurt, and Worcestershire sauce and simmer for 30 minutes. Serve hot or cold.   *Makes 1 cup.*

Each tablespoon has
3 grams of complete protein
57 calories

Barbecue Sauce

2 tablespoons safflower oil
2 tablespoons wine vinegar
1 cup tomato puree
2 tablespoons Worcestershire sauce
½ cup water
½ cup soy powder
1 clove garlic, minced
2 onions, finely chopped
1 teaspoon dry mustard
4 ripe tomatoes
1 teaspoon granulated sugar substitute
⅛ teaspoon cayenne pepper
½ teaspoon sea salt
½ teaspoon chili powder

Put safflower oil, vinegar, tomato puree, Worcester-shire sauce, and water in blender and mix for 10 seconds. Add soy powder, garlic, onions, dry mustard, tomatoes, sugar substitute, cayenne pepper, sea salt, and chili powder and blend for 30 seconds. Pour into pan and bring to boil, stirring constantly. Simmer for 10 minutes. Serve hot or cold.   *Makes 3 cups.*

Each cup has
7 grams of complete protein
251 calories

Onion Sauce

6 large onions, chopped finely
2 tablespoons safflower oil
1½ cups water
2 heaping tablespoons soy powder

*2 heaping tablespoons noninstant powdered skim
    milk
½ teaspoon sea salt
½ teaspoon paprika
4 tablespoons Worcestershire sauce
2 tablespoons soy sauce*

Cook chopped onions in safflower oil for 5 minutes until golden brown. Put water, soy powder, and powdered skim milk in blender for 30 seconds, then pour into pan with onions and add sea salt, paprika, worcestershire sauce, and soy sauce. Bring to boil, stirring constantly, and cook for 5 minutes. Serve hot or cold.   *Makes 2 cups.*

Each tablespoon has
2 grams of complete protein
25 calories

Pineapple Cheese Dressing

*1 cup unsweetened pineapple juice
½ cup orange juice
4 tablespoons lemon juice
1 tablespoon honey
1 cup cottage cheese
¼ teaspoon sea salt
½ cup noninstant powdered skim milk*

Put pineapple juice, orange juice, lemon juice, and honey in blender. Add cottage cheese, sea salt, and powdered skim milk. Pour over salad.   *Makes 2 ½ cups.*

Each ½ cup serving has
13 grams of complete protein
151 calories

Marvy Mayonnaise

2 eggs
2 tablespoons cider vinegar
½ cup safflower oil
½ teaspoon dry mustard
1 teaspoon sea salt
2 heaping tablespoons noninstant powdered skim
  milk
1 heaping tablespoon soy powder

Put eggs, vinegar, and oil in saucepan and beat until well mixed and smooth. Add dry mustard, sea salt, powdered skim milk, and soy powder, beating until blended. Cook over very low flame for 10 minutes. Cool and refrigerate. *Makes 1 cup.*

Each level tablespoon has
2 grams of complete protein
87 calories

Uncooked Mayonnaise

2 egg yolks
2 tablespoons lemon juice
2 tablespoons cider vinegar
1½ cups safflower oil
½ teaspoon sea salt
½ teaspoon dry mustard
¼ teaspoon paprika
2 heaping tablespoons soy powder
2 heaping tablespoons noninstant powdered skim
  milk

Put egg yolks, lemon juice, vinegar, and oil in blender. Add sea salt, mustard, paprika, soy powder, and powdered skim milk and blend 1 minute. Refrigerate.

Makes 2 cups.

Each tablespoon has
1 gram of complete protein
107 calories

Rosy Yogurt Dressing

1 cup yogurt
1 ripe tomato, cut up
4 tablespoons catsup
2 tablespoons safflower oil
⅛ teaspoon Tabasco sauce
¼ cup finely chopped onion
1 teaspoon granulated sugar substitute
2 heaping tablespoons noninstant powdered skim
    milk
2 heaping tablespoons soy powder
1 teaspoon sea salt
⅛ teaspoon pepper
½ cup water

Put yogurt, tomato, catsup, safflower oil, Tabasco sauce, onion, and sugar substitute in blender and mix for 30 seconds. Slowly add powdered skim milk, soy powder, sea salt, and pepper. Finally add water and blend for 30 more seconds.

Makes 2 cups.

Each cup has
18 grams of complete protein
401 calories

Fruit Topping

1 cup yogurt
2 tablespoons lemon juice
½ cup water
1 ripe avocado, diced
¼ teaspoon sea salt
⅛ teaspoon ginger
⅛ teaspoon cinnamon
1 teaspoon granulated sugar substitute
2 heaping tablespoons soy powder
2 heaping tablespoons noninstant powdered skim milk
1 tablespoon safflower oil

Put yogurt, lemon juice, water, and avocado in blender and mix for 30 seconds. Add sea salt, ginger, cinnamon, sugar substitute, soy powder, powdered skim milk, and safflower oil and blend another 30 seconds. Pour over sliced fruit.

Makes 2 cups.

Each cup has
18 grams of complete protein
412 calories

Mexican Chili Sauce

1 medium onion, chopped
1 garlic clove, minced
1 green pepper, chopped
2 tablespoons safflower oil
4 heaping tablespoons soy powder
4 heaping tablespoons noninstant powdered skim milk

½ teaspoon sea salt
1 tablespoon chili powder
2 cups tomatoes, cut up
4 egg yolks
1 cup water
1 teaspoon Tabasco sauce
½ teaspoon pepper

Sauté onion, garlic, and green pepper in oil until tender. Blend in soy powder, powdered skim milk, sea salt, and chili powder and stir till smooth. Slowly add tomatoes, egg yolks, water, Tabasco sauce, and pepper and cook till thickened, stirring constantly. Serve hot or cold. Keeps for 2 weeks in fridge in covered jar, or can be frozen and kept indefinitely. Pour 2 cups into ice tray, freeze, and as you need it, take the cubes out, heat, and use. *Makes 3 cups.*

Each cup has
23 grams of complete protein
384 calories

Red Relish

2 tablespoons lemon juice
1 tablespoon safflower oil
½ cup tomato juice
2 large cooked beets, diced
4 tablespoons horseradish
2 teaspoons sea salt
1 onion, chopped
1 teaspoon paprika
½ teaspoon granulated sugar substitute
2 heaping tablespoons soy powder

Put lemon juice, oil, tomato juice, beets, and horseradish in blender and mix for 10 seconds. Add sea salt, onion, paprika, sugar substitute, and soy powder and blend for 20 seconds. Refrigerate.   *Makes 1 cup.*

1 tablespoon has
1 gram of complete protein
23 calories

Cottage Salad Dressing

1 cup yogurt
1 cup tomato sauce
4 tablespoons safflower oil
¼ cup water
1 cup cottage cheese with chives
4 tablespoons chopped onion
2 tablespoons Worcestershire sauce
1 tablespoon soy sauce
2 heaping tablespoons noninstant powdered skim milk
1 clove garlic
1 teaspoon sea salt
⅛ teaspoon cayenne pepper

Put yogurt, tomato sauce, oil, and water in blender and add cottage cheese, onion, Worcestershire sauce, soy sauce, powdered skim milk, garlic, sea salt, and cayenne pepper. Blend for 1 minute. Pour over salad.   *Makes 3 cups.*

Each cup has
21 grams of complete protein
391 calories

Bleu Cheese Dressing

 1 tablespoon lemon juice
 1 tablespoon cider vinegar
 8 tablespoons safflower oil
 1 large ripe tomato, cut up
 2 tablespoons catsup
 ¼ cup water
 ½ cup crumbled bleu cheese
 1 clove garlic, minced
 ½ teaspoon sea salt
 ½ teaspoon paprika
 1 heaping tablespoon noninstant powdered skim
     milk
 1 heaping tablespoon soy powder
 ½ teaspoon dry mustard
 ½ cup skim milk cottage cheese

Put lemon juice, vinegar, oil, tomato, catsup, and water in blender and mix for 10 seconds. Add bleu cheese, garlic, sea salt, paprika, powdered skim milk, soy powder, dry mustard, and cottage cheese and blend for 45 seconds. Pour over salad.

Makes 1 ½ cups.

Each tablespoon has
3 grams of complete protein
69 calories

Tarragon Sauce

1 cup water
2 tablespoons safflower oil
4 egg yolks
½ cup tarragon vinegar
1 tablespoon Worcestershire sauce
1 clove garlic
2 tablespoons tarragon
1 tablespoon dry mustard
1 tablespoon chives
3 heaping tablespoons soy powder
1 teaspoon sea salt
1 teaspoon pepper

Put water, oil, egg yolks, vinegar, and Worcestershire sauce in blender and mix for 20 seconds. Add garlic, tarragon, mustard, chives, soy powder, sea salt, and pepper and blend for 30 seconds. Pour into saucepan and simmer for 10 minutes, stirring constantly. Serve hot or cold. *Makes 2 cups.*

Each cup has
17 grams of complete protein
349 calories

Red and Green Relish

4 large green peppers, minced
4 large red peppers, minced
2 large onions, minced
½ teaspoon sea salt
2 heaping tablespoons soy powder
1 tablespoon chopped chives

¼ cup apple cider vinegar
¼ teaspoon marjoram
¼ teaspoon tarragon
¼ teaspoon ground cloves
⅛ teaspoon Tabasco sauce
¼ teaspoon allspice

Put green peppers, red peppers, onions, sea salt, soy powder, chives, and vinegar in saucepan, bring to a boil and simmer for 10 minutes. Add marjoram, tarragon, cloves, Tabasco sauce, and allspice, mix well, and simmer another 3 minutes. Serve either hot or cold.   *Makes 2 cups.*

Each cup has
7 grams of complete protein
194 calories

Hard-Egg Salad Dressing

½ cup safflower oil
1 tomato, cut up
2 tablespoons wine vinegar
2 tablespoons chopped onion
2 tablespoons catsup
¼ cup water
1 teaspoon sea salt
1 teaspoon paprika
1 teaspoon dry mustard
1 heaping tablespoon soy powder
1 heaping tablespoon noninstant powdered skim
    milk
2 hard-cooked eggs, diced

Put oil, tomato, vinegar, onion, catsup, and water in blender and mix for 30 seconds. Add sea salt, paprika, mustard, soy powder, powdered skim milk, and eggs and blend another 30 seconds. Pour over salad. *Makes 1 ¼ cups.*

Each tablespoon has
1 gram of complete protein
69 calories

Moscow Dressing

½ cup safflower oil
1 tablespoon Worcestershire sauce
8 tablespoons catsup
1 tablespoon apple cider vinegar
1 tablespoon lemon juice
8 tablespoons water
1 onion, chopped finely
½ teaspoon sea salt
½ teaspoon paprika
1 teaspoon celery seed
1 teaspoon granulated sugar substitute
2 heaping tablespoons soy powder
2 heaping tablespoons noninstant powdered skim milk

Put safflower oil, Worcestershire sauce, catsup, vinegar, lemon juice, water, and onion in blender and mix for 30 seconds. Add sea salt, paprika, celery seed, sugar substitute, soy powder, and powdered skim milk and blend for 10 seconds. Pour over salad. *Makes 1 ½ cups.*

Each level tablespoon has
1 gram of complete protein
64 calories

Cucumber Salad Topping

2 tablespoons lemon juice
2 tablespoons chopped onion
1 cup yogurt
2 tablespoons safflower oil
1 large cucumber, peeled and diced
2 tablespoons chopped celery
2 tablespoons chopped parsley
2 heaping tablespoons noninstant powdered skim
    milk
1 heaping tablespoon soy powder
1 teaspoon sea salt
1 teaspoon pepper
½ teaspoon coriander seed
¼ cup water

Put lemon juice, onion, yogurt, oil, and cucumber into blender and mix for 30 seconds. Add celery, parsley, powdered skim milk, soy powder, sea salt, pepper, coriander seed, and water and blend for 30 more seconds. Pour over salad.

Makes 1 ½ cups.

Each ½ cup has
10 grams of complete protein
219 calories

Buttermilk Dressing

2 egg yolks
½ cup safflower oil
½ cup buttermilk
1 tablespoon Worcestershire sauce
½ teaspoon sea salt
½ teaspoon dry mustard
¼ teaspoon pepper
¼ teaspoon curry powder
¼ teaspoon turmeric
2 heaping tablespoons noninstant powdered skim
    milk
1 heaping tablespoon soy powder
¼ cup water

Put egg yolks, oil, buttermilk, and Worcestershire sauce in blender and mix for 30 seconds. Add sea salt, mustard, pepper, curry powder, turmeric, powdered skim milk, soy powder, and water and blend for another 30 seconds. Pour over salad.

Makes 1 ½ cups.

Each ½ cup has
10 grams of complete protein
474 calories

Raisin Yogurt Dressing

2 cups yogurt
1 tablespoon lemon juice
2 tablespoons safflower oil
1 tablespoon honey
¼ cup raisins

1 teaspoon granulated sugar substitute
2 heaping tablespoons soy powder
2 heaping tablespoons noninstant powdered skim
milk
¼ teaspoon sea salt
4 tablespoons water

Put yogurt, lemon juice, safflower oil, honey, and raisins in blender and mix for 30 seconds. Add sugar substitute, soy powder, powdered skim milk, sea salt, and water and blend another 30 seconds. Pour over salad. *Makes 2 cups.*

Each cup has
22 grams of complete protein
484 calories

Honey Dressing

½ cup safflower oil
2 eggs
4 tablespoons honey
5 tablespoons cider vinegar
1 tablespoon lemon juice
1 teaspoon granulated sugar substitute
1 teaspoon dry mustard
1 teaspoon sea salt
1 teaspoon paprika
1 teaspoon celery seed
2 heaping tablespoons soy powder
2 heaping tablespoons noninstant powdered skim
milk
¼ cup water

Put safflower oil, eggs, honey, vinegar, lemon juice, and sugar substitute in blender and mix for 10 seconds. Add mustard, sea salt, paprika, celery seed, soy powder, powdered skim milk, and water and blend for 30 seconds. Pour over salad.

Makes 1 ½ cups.

1 tablespoon has
2 grams of complete protein
64 calories

CHAPTER

8

Let 'em Eat Cake, Pies, and Cookies

FLOURLESS, LOW-CAL, HIGH-PROTE BAKED THINGS

JUST AS PAVLOV trained his animals, I trained myself (only in reverse). I learned to un-salivate, not at the sound of a bell, but at the sight of coffee ice cream, chocolate cheese cake, baba au rhum, and all the other unhealth-ful, low-prote, high-cal "badies."

For a while, all this un-salivating kept me dry mouthed and with my discipline satisfied but my taste definitely unsatisfied. Then my imagination tuned up to full power with the idea that with sugar substitutes and a lot of really good ingredients, I could whip up some "foolers."

135

I started by inventing a recipe for Molasses Fruit Cookies using no flour. They were so great all my friends ate them up in one sitting. Each cookie has 4 protein grams and 63 calories. Wrap five cookies, stick them in your pocket or purse, and eat them for lunch with a glass of skim milk and you'll have 29 protein grams and only 405 calories. *Twenty-nine* protein grams! That's 9 more than an average serving of steak, and one calorie less than 5 eggs. That'll keep you goin' with plenty of energy to last till dinner time.

Next I tried some Chocolate Cheese Cookies that knocked everybody out. They're chunky and chewy and cheesy like minia- ture cheese cakes and easy to make. Each cookie has 6 grams of prote and 79 cals. As soon as the crowd polished 'em off, I knew I had a good thing going.

I kept on inventing and really wowed 'em with Rum Chiffon Cheese Cake. I won a dollar bet from a buddy who insisted that it *had* to be loaded with sugar. Now that he knows me better, he'd bet a thousand dollars in the other direction. Each slice has 18 grams of prote and only 217 cals.

If you're a coco-nut, you'll go wild over the Macaroonys— everybody does. You'll get 2 grams of prote and 58 cals per Macaroony, and probably lose weight from all the chewing (great double-chin exercise!).

If Marie Antoinette had had these recipes, she probably would not have lost her head. Instead, when she mumbled "Let 'em eat cake," she would have been sainted.

Coffee Meringue Pie

    4 eggs
    1 cup skim milk
    ½ cup skim milk cottage cheese
    2 tablespoons safflower oil
    4 tablespoons honey
    1⅓ teaspoons granulated sugar substitute
    1 tablespoon coffee (or coffee substitute)
    1 tablespoon noninstant powdered skim milk
    1 tablespoon soy powder
    ½ teaspoon sea salt
    1 cup yogurt
    1 teaspoon granulated sugar substitute
    2 tablespoons honey
    1 baked Easy-Does-It Wheat-Germ Crust
       (Page 138)

Separate eggs. Put egg yolks and milk in blender. Add cottage cheese, oil, and honey and blend for 1 minute. Add sugar substitute, coffee, powdered skim milk, soy powder, and sea salt and blend for 30 seconds. Pour into pan and cook over low flame till slightly thickened. Pour into baked Easy-Does-It Wheat-Germ Crust and chill in fridge. Beat egg whites till stiff. Mix yogurt, sugar substitute, and honey in bowl and fold in egg whites. Cover pie completely with meringue and bake in very hot oven (500°) until golden brown, about 3 minutes.

Makes 8 slices.

Each slice has
15 grams of complete protein
389 calories

Easy-Does-It Wheat-Germ Crust

½ cup wheat germ (untoasted)
½ cup whole wheat flour (stone ground)
½ cup noninstant powdered skim milk
½ teaspoon sea salt
8 tablespoons safflower oil
1 tablespoon blackstrap molasses
1 tablespoon honey

Combine wheat germ, whole wheat flour, powdered skim milk, and sea salt in large bowl. Add oil, molasses, and honey, blend well, and mold into a pie tin. Bake in preheated oven at 425° for 10 minutes. *Makes 8-slice pie crust.*

Each slice has
6 grams of complete protein
237 calories

Rum Cream Pie

1 cup skim milk
1 cup yogurt
4 eggs
1 tablespoon safflower oil
4 tablespoons honey
½ cup skim milk cottage cheese
½ teaspoon sea salt
1 teaspoon rum flavor
2 teaspoons granulated sugar substitute
1 baked Easy-Does-It Wheat-Germ Crust
    (See above)

Put skim milk, yogurt, eggs, safflower oil, and honey in blender and mix for 1 minute. Add cottage cheese, sea salt, rum flavor, and sugar substitute and blend for 1 more minute. Pour into pan and cook over very low heat till mixture thickens. Pour into baked Easy-Does-It Wheat-Germ Crust. Chill and serve.

Makes 8 slices.

Each slice has
17 grams of complete protein
389 calories

Pumpkin Seed Pie

1½ cups cooked pumpkin
⅔ cup pumpkin seeds, chopped
3 teaspoons granulated sugar substitute
4 tablespoons honey
½ cup noninstant powdered skim milk
2 tablespoons safflower oil
½ teaspoon sea salt
½ teaspoon ginger
1 teaspoon cinnamon
¼ teaspoon nutmeg
4 eggs
1 cup skim milk
1 baked Easy-Does-It Wheat-Germ Crust
  (Page 138)

Combine pumpkin, pumpkin seeds, sugar substitute, honey, powdered skim milk, oil, sea salt, ginger, cinnamon, and nutmeg. Beat eggs and milk together in a separate bowl and add to mixture, blending well. Pour into Easy-Does-It Wheat-

Germ Crust and bake at 450° for 10 minutes, then 325°f. for about 45 minutes. Insert knife into center of pie. If it comes out clean, pie is done. *Makes 8 slices.*

Each slice has
17 grams of complete protein
460 calories

Pecan Maple Cream Pie

1 cup Maple Molasses Syrup (Chapter 7)
3 eggs
½ cup skim milk cottage cheese
½ cup noninstant powdered skim milk
1⅔ teaspoons granulated sugar substitute
¼ teaspoon sea salt
2 tablespoons honey
1 tablespoon safflower oil
1 cup pecans, chopped
1 baked Easy-Does-It Wheat-Germ Crust
    (Page 138)

Put Maple Molasses Syrup in blender. Add eggs, cottage cheese, powdered skim milk, sugar substitute, sea salt, honey, and oil. Blend for 1 minute. Pour into pan and cook over low flame until mixture thickens. Add ½ cup of pecans to mixture and stir well. Pour into baked Easy-Does-It Wheat-Germ Crust. Sprinkle remaining ½ cup pecans on top of pie. Chill and serve.
Makes 8 slices.

Each slice has
18 grams of complete protein
468 calories

Pumpkin Seed Cake

1 cup soy powder
½ cup noninstant powdered skim milk
1 cup soy grits
½ cup wheat germ (untoasted)
6 eggs
4 tablespoons safflower oil
3 teaspoons granulated sugar substitute
½ teaspoon sea salt
4 tablespoons honey
1 cup pumpkin seeds, chopped

Mix soy powder, powdered skim milk, soy grits, and wheat germ. In a separate bowl beat eggs, oil, sugar substitute, sea salt, honey, and pumpkin seeds. Pour into dry mixture and blend thoroughly. Bake in teflon-lined loaf pan at 350° for about 45 minutes or until golden brown. *Makes 10 slices.*

Each slice has
23 grams of complete protein
363 calories

Almond Cake

6 eggs
1⅓ teaspoons granulated sugar substitute
4 tablespoons honey
½ cup whole wheat pastry flour
¾ cup soy powder
¼ cup noninstant powdered skim milk
6 tablespoons safflower oil
1 tablespoon almond extract

Beat eggs, sugar substitute, and honey with rotary beater until foamy. Stir in whole wheat flour, soy powder, and powdered skim milk, mixing well. Add oil and stir in almond extract. Bake at 375° for about 25 minutes until golden brown.

Makes 8 slices.

Each slice has
10 grams of complete protein
232 calories

No-Flour Cake

1 cup soy powder
½ cup wheat germ (untoasted)
½ cup noninstant powdered skim milk
1 cup sunflower seeds
½ cup sesame seeds
3 teaspoons granulated sugar substitute
4 eggs
2 tablespoons safflower oil
4 tablespoons honey
1 teaspoon sea salt
skim milk, if needed

Mix soy powder, wheat germ, powdered skim milk, sunflower seeds, sesame seeds, and sugar substitute. In a separate bowl mix eggs, oil, honey, and salt. Pour into dry mixture and blend well. If too dry, add skim milk by the tablespoon until blendable, but still very firm. Bake in teflon-lined loaf pan at 350° for 45 minutes or until golden brown.   *Makes 10 slices.*

Each slice has
16 grams of complete protein
286 calories

Banana Cake

2 eggs
4 tablespoons safflower oil
3 teaspoons granulated sugar substitute
4 tablespoons honey
½ teaspoon sea salt
1 teaspoon vanilla
½ teaspoon soda
¼ cup yogurt
1 cup banana pulp
½ cup whole wheat pastry flour
¼ cup wheat germ
1 cup soy powder
¼ cup noninstant powdered skim milk

Mix eggs, oil, sugar substitute, honey, sea salt, vanilla, soda, yogurt, and banana pulp. Blend thoroughly. In a separate bowl mix whole wheat flour, wheat germ, soy powder, and powdered skim milk, then add to liquid mixture. Beat well and pour into teflon-lined loaf pan. Bake at 350° for 45 minutes or until golden brown.   *Makes 8 slices.*

Each slice has
10 grams of complete protein
235 calories

Chocolate Mint Chiffon Cheese Cake

4 eggs
1 tablespoon safflower oil
4 tablespoons honey
2½ cups cottage cheese
1 level tablespoon cocoa (no sugar)
3⅓ teaspoons granulated sugar substitute
1 cup soy powder
1 cup noninstant powdered skim milk
½ cup wheat germ (untoasted)
½ teaspoon sea salt
½ teaspoon mint flavor

Separate eggs. Put yolks, oil, and honey in blender. Add cottage cheese and blend for 1 minute. Pour into large bowl and add cocoa, sugar substitute, soy powder, powdered skim milk, wheat germ, sea salt, and mint flavor, blending well. Beat egg whites till stiff and fold into mixture. Pour into pan that has removable sides. Bake for 1¼ hours at 325°. Cool before removing sides. Chill in fridge. *Makes 10 slices.*

Each slice has
23 grams of complete protein
224 calories

Rum Chiffon Cheese Cake

4 eggs
1 cup yogurt
3 cups cottage cheese
4 tablespoons honey
2 tablespoons safflower oil
1 tablespoon lemon juice

1 teaspoon rum flavor
¼ teaspoon sea salt
3 teaspoons granulated sugar substitute
4 heaping tablespoons noninstant powdered skim milk
½ cup whole wheat pastry flour (stone ground)

Separate eggs. Put yolks and yogurt in blender. Add cottage cheese, honey, oil, lemon juice, and rum flavor. Pour into bowl. Add sea salt, sugar substitute, powdered skim milk, and pastry flour, blending well. Beat egg whites till stiff and fold into mixture. Pour into pan that has removable sides. Bake at 300° for 1½ hours. Then let cool before removing sides. Chill in fridge.

Makes 10 slices.

Each slice has
18 grams of complete protein
217 calories

Roquefort Cheese Cake

2 heaping tablespoons soy powder
2 heaping tablespoons noninstant powdered skim milk
3 teaspoons granulated sugar substitute
2 cups skim milk cottage cheese
½ cup Roquefort cheese, packed solidly
3 eggs
½ cup yogurt
¼ teaspoon sea salt
2 teaspoons grated lemon rind
4 tablespoons honey
fresh strawberries, crushed

Combine soy powder and powdered skim milk. Add sugar substitute, cottage cheese, and roquefort cheese and mix until smooth. Beat eggs, yogurt, sea salt, lemon rind, and honey into mixture and stir until smooth. Pour into pan and bake at 300° for 45 minutes. Turn off heat and let sit in oven 1 hour more. Top with crushed fresh strawberries.   *Makes 10 slices.*

Each slice has
17 grams of complete protein
145 calories

Pineapple Cheese Cake

2 eggs
1 cup skim milk cottage cheese
2 cups crushed diet pineapple (no sugar, no liquid)
2 tablespoons safflower oil
4 tablespoons honey
½ teaspoon vanilla
½ teaspoon sea salt
½ cup wheat germ (untoasted)
1 cup soy powder
1 cup noninstant powdered skim milk
3 teaspoons granulated sugar substitute

Put eggs, cottage cheese, pineapple, and safflower oil in blender for 1 minute. Pour into bowl and add honey, vanilla, sea salt, wheat germ, soy powder, powdered skim milk, and sugar substitute, mixing well. Pour into loaf pan and bake at 325° for 1 hour, or until golden brown on top.   *Makes 10 slices.*

Each slice has
18 grams of complete protein
202 calories

Italian Cheese Cake

>2 pounds ricotta cheese
>½ cup yogurt
>2 tablespoons lemon juice
>1 tablespoon grated lemon rind
>1 teaspoon vanilla
>3 teaspoons granulated sugar substitute
>8 tablespoons honey
>4 eggs
>¼ cup whole wheat pastry flour (stone ground)
>½ teaspoon sea salt
>1 tablespoon safflower oil

Combine ricotta cheese, yogurt, lemon juice, lemon rind, and vanilla in a large bowl. Add sugar substitute, honey, and eggs and blend well. Add pastry flour, sea salt, and oil and blend well. Pour into cheese-cake pan and bake at 300° for 1 hour. Turn off oven and let sit for 30 minutes more.   *Makes 8 slices.*

Each slice has
19 grams of complete protein
257 calories

Macaroonys

>3 cups shredded coconut, packed solidly
>½ cup soy powder
>½ cup noninstant powdered skim milk
>3 teaspoons granulated sugar substitute
>4 tablespoons honey
>1 teaspoon vanilla
>1 tablespoon safflower oil
>½ teaspoon sea salt
>1 cup skim milk

Put coconut in large bowl. Add soy powder, powdered skim milk, sugar substitute, honey, vanilla, oil, and salt. Slowly add skim milk and blend, but only enough milk to have mixture form firm balls. Put coconut balls on cookie sheet and bake at 375° for about 6 minutes in a preheated oven until lightly browned. *Makes 35 cookies.*

Each cookie has
2 grams of complete protein
58 calories

Chocolate Cheese Cookies

½ cup wheat germ (untoasted)
1 cup soy powder
3⅓ teaspoons granulated sugar substitute
1 level tablespoon cocoa (no sugar)
4 heaping tablespoons noninstant powdered skim milk
½ cup raisins
1 cup skim milk cottage cheese
2 eggs
2 tablespoons safflower oil
3 tablespoons honey

Mix wheat germ, soy powder, sugar substitute, cocoa, powdered skim milk, and raisins in a large bowl. Add cottage cheese, eggs, oil, and honey, blending well. Drop on cookie sheet and bake for 12 minutes at 350° in preheated oven. *Makes 32 cookies.*

Each cookie has
6 grams of complete protein
79 calories

Spicy Raisin Drops

½ cup whole wheat flour (stone ground)
½ cup soy powder
½ cup wheat germ (untoasted)
½ cup noninstant powdered skim milk
½ teaspoon sea salt
½ teaspoon cinnamon
½ teaspoon cloves
¼ teaspoon ginger
1⅓ teaspoons granulated sugar substitute
1 cup raisins
½ cup sunflower seeds
1 cup yogurt
6 tablespoons safflower oil
1 tablespoon cider vinegar
2 tablespoons honey

Mix whole wheat flour, soy powder, wheat germ, and powdered skim milk. Add sea salt, cinnamon, cloves, ginger, and sugar substitute, mixing well. Add raisins and sunflower seeds. In another bowl mix yogurt, oil, vinegar, and honey. Add liquid slowly to dry mixture, stirring well. Drop by teaspoon on cookie sheet. Bake at 350° for about 15 minutes until lightly browned.

Makes 40 cookies.

Each cookie has
2 grams of complete protein
69 calories

Honey Almond Crunchers

    1 cup soy powder
    ½ cup soy grits
    ½ cup wheat germ (untoasted)
    ½ cup noninstant powdered skim milk
    ½ cup whole wheat flour (stone ground)
    3 teaspoons granulated sugar substitute
    ½ cup chopped almonds
    1 cup sunflower seeds
    6 eggs
    4 tablespoons safflower oil
    4 tablespoons honey
    ½ teaspoon sea salt

Combine soy powder, soy grits, wheat germ, powdered skim milk, whole wheat flour, and sugar substitute. Add
chopped almonds and sunflower seeds. Blend in eggs, oil, honey,
and sea salt and mix well. Drop on cookie sheet and bake at 350°
for about 15 minutes or until golden brown. *Makes 60 cookies.*

    Each cookie has
    3 grams of complete protein
    72 calories

Light and Dark Crunchers

    1 cup soy grits
    1 cup soy powder
    1 cup noninstant powdered skim milk
    ½ cup wheat germ (untoasted)
    1 cup sunflower seeds
    ½ cup sesame seeds

3⅓ teaspoons sugar substitute
½ cup raisins
6 eggs
¼ cup safflower oil
1 teaspoon sea salt
4 tablespoons honey
4 tablespoons blackstrap molasses

Combine soy grits, soy powder, powdered skim milk, wheat germ, sunflower seeds, sesame seeds, sugar substitute, and raisins. Add eggs, oil, and sea salt and blend well. Put mixture in 2 separate bowls. Add honey to one bowl and blend well. Add blackstrap molasses to the other bowl and blend well. Each bowl makes 40 cookies. Drop by spoonful on cookie sheet and bake at 350° for 12 minutes or until browned.   *Makes 80 cookies.*

Each cookie has
3 grams of complete protein
59 calories

Raisin Bran Muffins

½ cup whole wheat flour
¼ cup wheat germ (untoasted)
1 cup soy powder
¼ cup noninstant powdered skim milk
1 teaspoon sea salt
4 teaspoons granulated sugar substitute
2 eggs
2 tablespoons safflower oil
1½ cups skim milk
2 cups whole bran
½ cup raisins

Mix whole wheat flour, wheat germ, soy powder, powdered skim milk, sea salt, and sugar substitute. Mix eggs, oil, skim milk and add to flour. Add bran and raisins and stir. Let stand for 2 minutes. Stir again. Fill muffin tins ⅔ full. Bake at 350° for 30 minutes or until lightly brown.   *Makes 24 muffins.*

Each muffin has
4 grams of complete protein
79 calories

Molasses Fruit Cookies

2 cups soy powder
1 cup noninstant powdered skim milk
½ cup wheat germ (untoasted)
3⅓ teaspoons granulated sugar substitute
½ teaspoon sea salt
½ cup sunflower seeds
4 eggs
4 tablespoons safflower oil
3 tablespoons molasses
1¼ cups mixed chopped fruit (blueberries, apples, peaches, etc.)
½ cup raisins

Combine soy powder, powdered skim milk, wheat germ, sugar substitute, sea salt, and sunflower seeds. Blend in eggs, oil, molasses, chopped fruit, and raisins, mixing well. Drop by spoonful onto cookie sheet and bake at 325° for 20 minutes or until browned.   *Makes 50 cookies.*

Each cookie has
4 grams of complete protein
63 calories

Molasses Nut Bread

4 eggs
1⅓ teaspoons granulated sugar substitute
4 tablespoons safflower oil
10 tablespoons blackstrap molasses
1 cup yogurt
½ cup whole wheat flour
1 teaspoon sea salt
1 teaspoon soda
1¾ cups soy powder
¼ cup wheat germ (untoasted)
½ cup soy grits
½ cup sunflower seeds
1 cup chopped English walnuts
1 cup raisins

Beat eggs and sugar substitute until slightly thickened. Add oil, molasses, and yogurt and mix well. Add whole wheat flour mixed with sea salt and soda, then add soy powder and wheat germ. Beat till smooth. Fold in soy grits, sunflower seeds, walnuts, and raisins and blend well. Bake in teflon-lined pan at 350° for 1 hour.   *Makes 16 slices.*

Each slice has
11 grams of complete protein
259 calories

Molasses Puffins

        1 egg
        4 tablespoons blackstrap molasses
        ¾ cup yogurt
        4 tablespoons safflower oil
        ¼ teaspoon sea salt
        1 teaspoon soda
        1 teaspoon ginger
        ½ teaspoon cinnamon
        ¼ teaspoon nutmeg
        ¾ cup whole wheat flour (stone ground)
        ¾ cup soy powder
        4 tablespoons wheat germ (untoasted)
        4 heaping tablespoons noninstant powdered skim
            milk

Mix egg, molasses, yogurt, oil, salt, soda, ginger, cinnamon, and nutmeg. Blend well. In a separate bowl mix whole wheat flour, soy powder, wheat germ, and powdered skim milk. Add this to molasses mixture and blend thoroughly. Fill oiled cupcake pans ½ full. Bake for 20 minutes at 350°

Makes 12 puffins.

        Each puffin has
        7 grams of complete protein
        165 calories

Pineapple Zingers

        2 cups soy powder
        1 cup noninstant powdered skim milk
        1 cup wheat germ (untoasted)

½ cup sesame seeds
1 cup sunflower seeds
½ cup raisins
4 teaspoons granulated sugar substitute
4 eggs
2 tablespoons safflower oil
1½ cups crushed pineapple (no sugar, no juice)
½ teaspoon sea salt
pineapple juice, if needed

Mix soy powder, powdered skim milk, wheat germ, sesame seeds, sunflower seeds, raisins, and sugar substitute. Add eggs, oil, pineapple, and sea salt and mix well. If mixture is dry, add pineapple juice by the teaspoon until moist enough. Drop onto cookie sheet and bake at 350° for 12 minutes or until browned on top.   *Makes 80 cookies.*

Each cookie has
3 grams of complete protein
48 calories

No-Knead Easy-Does-It Yeast Bread

2 cups water
1 cup quick cooking steel-cut oatmeal
6 tablespoons safflower oil
6 tablespoons honey
4 teaspoons sea salt
2 cakes baker's yeast or 2 packages granular baking
    yeast
2 eggs
3 cups whole wheat flour (stone ground)
½ cup wheat germ
2 cups soy powder

Boil water and take off flame. Add oatmeal, oil, honey, and sea salt and stir until lukewarm. Add yeast and mix well. Beat eggs and blend into mixture. Add whole wheat flour, wheat germ, and soy powder, mixing till dough is well blended. Place in large oiled bowl and cover with waxed paper. Let sit in fridge at least 2 hours or more. When ready, shape 2 loaves. Place in 2 oiled pans 9 X 4 X 3 inches and cover. Let rise in warm place for 2 hours. Bake at 375° for 1 hour.   *Makes 2 loaves.*

Each loaf has
56 grams of complete protein
1992 calories

Raisin Cheese Bread

¾ cup water
1 cup raisins
¾ cup whole wheat flour (stone ground)
¾ cup soy powder
¼ cup wheat germ
¼ teaspoon sea salt
1 teaspoon soda
1 teaspoon granulated sugar substitute
4 tablespoons honey
1 egg
1 cup grated Cheddar cheese
1 cup sunflower seeds

Boil water and put raisins in it. In a separate bowl mix whole wheat flour, soy powder, wheat germ, salt, soda, and sugar substitute. Add raisin mixture, honey, egg, cheese, and sunflower seeds. Mix well. Bake in teflon-lined loaf pan at 350° for about 45 minutes, or until browned on top.   *Makes 10 slices.*

Each slice has
12 grams of complete protein
285 calories

9

Low-Cal Yummies for No-Fat Tummies

HIGH-PROTE DESSERTS THAT *MUST* BE FATTENING—BUT THEY'RE NOT

ALMOST EVERYBODY in New York knows Moondog. He's blind (from World War II, he says), wears sandals, a headdress, and long flowing robes, and looks as if he just stepped out of a Wagnerian opera. At about six feet five inches, he's an imposing figure standing on the corner of Sixth Avenue and Fifty-fifth Street. He's been there for years and tourists love him. Most just stand back and stare, but the brave go right up and talk. One day I lured him to the Opera Espresso, and from then on, for a minor amount of money and dinner, he stood every evening at our front door. People going to Lincoln Center crowded around him. He recited poems or delved into different philosophies with anyone interested in listening. He sort of became our mascot.

"Poison white sugar," he used to intone, and I began to think of him as a food faddist. I was just starting to learn a little of nutrition from what I felt was a logical viewpoint. I accepted nothing as a fact until I tried it out on myself. If it worked, great. If not, so what? At that time all the groovy desserts at the Opera Espresso were made with sugar. I mean, could you have a Caramello Caruso without sugar? Or a Strawberry Sutherland? Or a Gobbi Glog Nog? No chance, and I ate 'em all. I even invented flavored whipped cream, which went on various desserts. My all-time favorite dessert was Caramello Caruso (the sweetest thing I've ever tasted, and that's why it used to be my favorite), topped with rum whipped cream oozing down the sides. At this point of my life, I hit my all-time high on the scales (the number I never have and never will reveal), and it was absolutely incredible how much sugar I could gorge. "Poison white sugar" indeed! Moondog had to be a nut. I was eating the poison and I was still alive. Not until several years later did I begin to understand what he meant.

When I went to Buenos Aires to do the film, I needed to lose weight. Just being away from the Opera Espresso helped (try being surrounded by every mouth-watering yummy and not sampling—impossible!). To speed things up I decided to cut out all sugar. Between Buenos Aires and the film, TV appearances in Caracas and Rio de Janeiro, and a Brazilian movie, I spent almost two years in South America—two years without sugar. When I returned to New York, I went on a binge. I'd never before been off sugar, so now, gorging myself, I felt exactly what it did to me. All of a sudden tension spread through me. For the first few minutes I felt more alert, but the more I ate the tenser I became, like a tightly wound coil. A day of this and I was so jumpy I felt like screaming. So I cut out the sugar to see what would happen, and I unwound. I found out that sugar *is* a poison. You can prove it to yourself, and it's worthwhile to find out. Cut out *all* sugar and booze and starchy foods (alcohol, bread, cakes, and starchy vegetables such as potatoes turn to sugar in your mouth) for ten days, and up your prote (which is *real* energy food). You'll feel yourself unwind and become less jumpy and irritable. You'll also find you'll have lots more energy to *use* instead of wasting it on tension. Then on the eleventh day gorge yourself with candy, cake, etc. You'll feel it all right.

The B vitamins in your body (which keep you calm) are used up in burning sugar, and the more sugar your body burns, the more B vitamins you need. Your requirement of the B vites is in direct proportion to the amount of carbohydrates, or sugar, you eat. So sugar robs the B vites from your body. No wonder I was nervous as a kid.

Sugar is responsible for many ills, including heart attacks. How many years do you think the body can stand being robbed of the B vites and not suffer? People eat so much sugar because advertisers have brainwashed them to believe it's the only energy food, that it's essential for energy. But that is *not* true. Sugar gives you a fast, short, unlasting lift, then drops you lower than before. High-protein foods give you TRUE ENERGY with no letdown.

No wonder people become depressed and jumpy. They have "sugar hangovers." And the awful part is that the more sugar you eat, the more you crave. SUGAR IS ADDICTIVE. Just like booze and nicotine and drugs—and it has no nutritional value at all. *But,* the less sugar you eat, the less you crave.

I made up my mind a long time ago that feeling good was the most important thing in my life, because when I felt lousy, everything I did was lousy, and who wants to go through life like that? I decided to give up the real pleasure (and it obviously *is* a real pleasure) of tasting sugary things, because it's only a temporary pleasure of a few minutes. I traded it for the longer-range energy and calmness that comes with food discipline. But if those few minutes of pleasure really mean a lot to you, go ahead. It's a slow process anyway, and it takes years to do the real damage.

When you stop eating refined sugar, you will truly begin to

have no craving. From fresh fruit you'll get a little natural sugar and more nutrition. From milk you'll get lactose (milk sugar), which is natural, unrefined, and nutritional.

If you like milk, you'll like yogurt. Why not make your own? It's better tasting and you'll save money. I eat a cup a day, and at today's prices (which keep going up), I saved $73 last year making my own. The yogurt maker is very inexpensive, only a few dollars. It's a small "warm plate" that holds four square glass dishes with lids. To make no-cal, flavored yogurt takes only a few minutes. Put 2 cups of whole milk and 2 of skim milk in a large pan and bring to a boil. Remove from heat and cool to lukewarm. Mix 3 teaspoons of the lukewarm milk with one teaspoon of yogurt (either fresh or from your last batch), then add to the boiled milk in the pan, stirring well. Use 1⅓ teaspoons of sugar substitute per batch (you make 4 cups at once), pour it into each dish, plug in the yogurt maker, and add a drop of a flavor. You can get strawberry, raspberry, maple, vanilla, rum, coffee, banana, pineapple—you name it. You can add the sugar substitute and flavor just before you eat it, but it's more fun this way. A heaping tablespoon of noninstant powdered skim milk added to the batch will make it creamier and add complete protein, so instead of 8 grams of prote per cup, you'll get 10 grams. And there's *no* refined sugar—just high prote and very low calories. It's my all-time "flavorite" dessert.

To help in giving up sugar, follow the recipes in this chapter. You'll be able to whip up some dishes that taste scrumptious and are really good for you. Try Peach Perfection, a dreamy, creamy dessert you'll fall in love with. If you serve eight small dishes, each dish will have 11 grams of protein and only 178 calories. If you want larger portions, serve four dishes and you'll get 23 grams of prote and only 356 cals.

In warm weather the Frozen Maple Cream is a dream. The recipe makes eight frozen-on-a-stick bars. Each one has 16 grams of protein and only 197 calories—and they taste as good as ice cream ever did!

The Rum Pumpkin Pudding is a snap to make in your blender. It contains pumpkin seeds for really great flavor. And they're good for you, with high amounts of B vites and minerals and perfect, complete protein. The pudding will give you 16 grams of prote and a low 246 cals.

Every dessert recipe here is a winner. And you can experiment with the amount of sugar substitutes you use. As you get healthier and your sugar craving lessens, you'll find you don't need so much sweetness. And the more prote you eat, the stronger, more energetic you'll feel, 'cause it's truly the *real* energy food.

Rum Pumpkin Pudding

½ cup skim milk
4 eggs
1 cup cottage cheese
4 tablespoons honey
2 tablespoons safflower oil
1 teaspoon rum flavor
1½ teaspoons granulated sugar substitute
½ teaspoon sea salt
¼ teaspoon nutmeg
½ teaspoon ginger
1 teaspoon cinnamon
2 heaping tablespoons noninstant powdered skim
    milk
2 heaping tablespoons soy powder
⅔ cup pumpkin seeds
1½ cups cooked pumpkin

Put milk and eggs in blender. Add cottage cheese, honey, oil, rum flavor, sugar substitute, sea salt, nutmeg, ginger, cinnamon, powdered skim milk, and soy powder. Blend 1 minute. Add pumpkin seeds and blend 10 seconds. Put pumpkin in large pan and add mixture, blending thoroughly. Cook slowly over very low heat until it bubbles and thickens, stirring constantly. Pour into dessert dishes and chill.   *Makes 8 servings.*

Each serving has
16 grams of complete protein
246 calories

Eggnog Pudding

4 eggs
1⅓ teaspoons granulated sugar substitute
⅛ teaspoon sea salt
⅛ teaspoon nutmeg
2 heaping tablespoons noninstant powdered skim
    milk
2 cups skim milk
½ teaspoon vanilla
1 tablespoon safflower oil
4 tablespoons honey

Separate eggs. Beat yolks, sugar substitute, sea salt, nutmeg, powdered skim milk, skim milk, vanilla, oil, and honey. Beat egg whites till stiff and fold into mixture. Cook over medium flame until mixture thickens. Pour into dessert dishes.

Makes 4 servings.

Each serving has
14 grams of complete protein
246 calories

Russian Chocolate Mint Pudding

2 eggs
1 cup skim milk
1 cup skim milk cottage cheese
1 tablespoon safflower oil
4 tablespoons honey
½ teaspoon peppermint extract
½ teaspoon vanilla

1 level tablespoon unsweetened cocoa or 3 table-
    spoons carob powder
1⅓ teaspoons granulated sugar substitute
¼ teaspoon sea salt
4 heaping tablespoons noninstant powdered skim
    milk

Separate eggs. Put egg yolks, skim milk, cottage
cheese, oil, honey, peppermint extract, and vanilla in blender and
mix for 1 minute. Add cocoa, sugar substitute, sea salt, and powdered skim milk and blend for 30 seconds. Pour into pan. Beat
egg whites till stiff and fold into mixture. Cook over very low heat
until thickened, stirring constantly. Pour into dessert dishes.

Makes 4 servings.

Each serving has
24 grams of complete protein
281 calories

Peanut Butter Pudding

2 cups skim milk
4 eggs
4 tablespoons peanut butter
¼ teaspoon vanilla
¼ teaspoon sea salt
1 teaspoon granulated sugar substitute
3 tablespoons honey
1 cup cottage cheese
2 heaping tablespoons noninstant powdered skim
    milk
1 heaping tablespoon soy powder

Put milk and eggs in blender for 30 seconds. Add peanut butter, vanilla, sea salt, sugar substitute, honey, cottage cheese, powdered skim milk, and soy powder. Blend for 45 seconds. Pour into pan and slowly bring to boil, stirring constantly. Cook over very low flame until mixture thickens (about 2 minutes). Pour into dessert dishes and chill.   *Makes 8 servings.*

Each serving has
13 grams of complete protein
180 calories

Italian Pudding

2 heaping tablespoons soy powder
1½ pounds ricotta cheese
4 tablespoons almonds, chopped
2 tablespoons pine nuts, chopped
2 tablespoons citron, chopped
4 eggs
1⅓ teaspoons granulated sugar substitute
2 tablespoons honey
¾ teaspoon vanilla
¾ teaspoon almond flavor
½ teaspoon sea salt
1 teaspoon safflower oil

Mix soy powder, cheese, almonds, pine nuts, and citron. In a separate bowl beat eggs and mix with sugar substitute, honey, vanilla, almond flavor, sea salt, and oil. Blend in with cheese and mix well. Pour into custard cups and bake at 375° for 30 minutes, or until firm.   *Makes 8 servings.*

Each serving has
17 grams of complete protein
208 calories

Raisin Cream

4 eggs
1 tablespoon safflower oil
⅛ teaspoon sea salt
¼ teaspoon cinnamon
¼ teaspoon nutmeg
½ teaspoon vanilla
1⅓ teaspoons granulated sugar substitute
2 tablespoons honey
1½ cups skim milk
2 tablespoons soy powder
4 tablespoons noninstant powdered skim milk
1 cup raisins
1 cup chopped walnuts

Separate eggs and put yolks in pan. Add oil, sea salt, cinnamon, nutmeg, vanilla, sugar substitute, honey, and skim milk. Mix well and cook over low flame till slightly thickened, stirring constantly. Add soy powder, powdered skim milk, raisins, and walnuts and stir till blended. Beat egg whites till stiff and fold in, stirring until creamy and thick. Pour into dessert dishes.

Makes 4 servings.

Each serving has
25 grams of complete protein
486 calories

Wheat Germ Pudding

1 cup skim milk
4 eggs
1 tablespoon safflower oil
2 tablespoons honey
½ cup wheat germ (untoasted)
½ cup noninstant powdered skim milk
½ teaspoon sea salt
1 teaspoon vanilla
¼ teaspoon nutmeg
1⅓ teaspoons granulated sugar substitute

Put skim milk, eggs, safflower oil, and honey in blender and mix for 30 seconds. Add wheat germ, powdered skim milk, sea salt, vanilla, nutmeg, and sugar substitute and blend for 1 minute. Pour into pan and cook over very low heat until thickened, stirring constantly. Pour into dessert dishes.

Makes 4 servings.

Each serving has
18 grams of complete protein
272 calories

Creamy Lemon Surprise

¼ cup stone-ground whole wheat flour
½ cup soy powder
1⅓ teaspoons granulated sugar substitute
⅛ teaspoon sea salt
2 tablespoons safflower oil
6 tablespoons lemon juice
2 tablespoons finely grated lemon peel

½ cup skim milk
1 cup yogurt
4 tablespoons honey
4 eggs

Mix whole wheat flour, soy powder, sugar substitute, sea salt, safflower oil, lemon juice, and lemon peel. In another bowl mix skim milk, yogurt, and honey. Separate eggs. Add yolks to milk, yogurt, and honey and blend well. Pour into dry mixture and stir until mixed thoroughly. Beat egg whites till stiff. Fold into mixture. Pour into shallow baking dish and bake in pan of hot water at 325° for 50 minutes.   *Makes 4 servings.*

Each serving has
16 grams of complete protein
322 calories

Mocha Cream

4 eggs
1 cup skim milk
1 tablespoon safflower oil
4 tablespoons honey
1 cup yogurt
½ cup cottage cheese
4 teaspoons Sanka or coffee substitute
1⅔ teaspoons granulated sugar substitute
¼ teaspoon sea salt
1 level tablespoon cocoa or 3 tablespoons carob
    powder
4 heaping tablespoons noninstant powdered skim
    milk

Put eggs, skim milk, safflower oil, honey, yogurt, and cottage cheese in blender for 1 minute. Add Sanka, sugar substitute, sea salt, cocoa, and powdered skim milk and blend 30 seconds. Pour into saucepan and cook over very low heat until thickened, stirring constantly. Pour into dessert dishes.

Makes 4 servings.

Each serving has
22 grams of complete protein
299 calories

Molasses Zing

> 4 eggs
> ½ cup blackstrap molasses
> 2 tablespoons honey
> 2 cups yogurt
> ½ teaspoon lemon rind, grated
> ⅛ teaspoon sea salt
> ¼ teaspoon ginger
> ¼ teaspoon cinnamon

Separate eggs. In a bowl beat the egg yolks until slightly thickened. In a pan mix molasses, honey, yogurt, lemon rind, sea salt, ginger, and cinnamon and bring to boil. Pour egg yolks very slowly into molasses mixture, beating constantly until slightly more thickened. In a large bowl beat the egg whites until stiff. Fold into molasses mixture, blending well, and cook over very low heat for just a few minutes until thickened. Serve hot or cold.

Makes 4 servings.

Each serving has
10 grams of complete protein
260 calories

Creamy Maple Rice

3 cups water
1½ teaspoons sea salt
½ cup uncooked brown rice
½ cup noninstant powdered skim milk
½ cup soy powder
¼ teaspoon nutmeg
1⅔ teaspoons granulated sugar substitute
½ cup raisins
1 cup skim milk
2 eggs
1 teaspoon maple flavor
2 tablespoons safflower oil
4 tablespoons honey

Bring water to boil and add sea salt and rice. Cover and simmer over very low flame until rice is cooked (about one hour.) When rice is done and all water absorbed, take off stove. In a bowl mix powdered skim milk, soy powder, nutmeg, sugar substitute, and raisins. To this mixture slowly add skim milk, mixing well. Beat in eggs, maple flavor, oil, and honey. Add rice and stir well. Pour into oiled baking dish and bake at 325° for 35 minutes.   *Makes 8 medium servings (or 4 large.)*

Each medium serving has
9 grams of complete protein
220 calories

Peach Perfection

1¼ cups skim milk
4 eggs
4 tablespoons honey
1 tablespoon safflower oil
4 tablespoons soy powder
4 tablespoons noninstant powdered skim milk
¼ teaspoon almond extract
1⅓ teaspoons granulated sugar substitute
⅛ teaspoon sea salt
2 cups sliced peaches
1 teaspoon lemon juice

Put milk, eggs, honey, oil, soy powder, powdered skim milk, almond extract, sugar substitute, and sea salt in blender and mix for 1 minute. Add peaches and lemon juice and blend for 10 seconds. Pour into large saucepan and cook over very low flame, stirring constantly till it begins to bubble and thicken. Pour into dessert dishes and chill. *Makes 4 servings.*

Each serving has
23 grams of complete protein
356 calories

Apple-cot Fluff

4 eggs
½ cup skim milk
1 tablespoon safflower oil
1 cup yogurt
8 apricots, cut up
1 apple, cut up

½ cup noninstant powdered skim milk
¼ cup soy powder
1⅓ teaspoons granulated sugar substitute
½ teaspoon sea salt
2 tablespoons honey
½ teaspoon vanilla

Separate eggs. Put yolks, skim milk, oil, and yogurt in blender and mix for 10 seconds. Add apricots and apple and blend for 30 seconds. Add powdered skim milk, soy powder, sugar substitute, sea salt, honey, and vanilla and blend for 45 seconds. Pour into saucepan. Beat egg whites till stiff and blend into mixture. Heat slowly till thickened, stirring constantly. Pour into dessert dishes. *Makes 4 servings.*

Each serving has
19 grams of complete protein
301 calories

Nut Nilsson

6 egg yolks
1 teaspoon granulated sugar substitute
2 tablespoons honey
4 heaping tablespoons soy powder
6 tablespoons Marsala wine
6 egg whites
½ cup chopped walnuts
1 teaspoon granulated sugar substitute
2 tablespoons honey

Separate eggs. In top of double boiler beat egg yolks until thick and creamy and add sugar substitute, honey, and soy powder. Beat for about 3 minutes and add Marsala wine, beating continually until lemon colored. Pour into bake-proof dishes and chill.

When ready to serve, put 6 egg whites in blender and beat till stiff. Add walnuts, sugar substitute, and honey. Pour atop pudding and put under high broiler for 3 minutes or until browned.

Makes 4 servings.

Each serving has
19 grams of complete protein
332 calories

Strawberry Cream

4 eggs
1 cup yogurt
1 cup fresh strawberries (or frozen without sugar)
1 tablespoon lemon juice
2 tablespoons honey
1 teaspoon vanilla
1 cup skim milk cottage cheese
¼ teaspoon sea salt
*4 heaping tablespoons noninstant powdered skim
    milk*
4 heaping tablespoons soy powder
1⅔ teaspoons granulated sugar substitute
1 tablespoon safflower oil

Put eggs, yogurt, and strawberries in blender. Add lemon juice, honey, vanilla, cottage cheese, and sea salt. Blend for 1 minute. Slowly add powdered skim milk, soy powder, and sugar substitute and mix another 45 seconds. Pour into saucepan and

cook slowly over very low flame until thickened, stirring constantly. Pour into dessert dishes.   *Makes 4 servings.*

Each serving has
34 grams of complete protein
342 calories

Frozen Maple Cream On-a-Stick

2 cups skim milk
1 cup cottage cheese
2 eggs
4 tablespoons honey
1 teaspoon maple flavor
1 tablespoon safflower oil
4 heaping tablespoons noninstant powdered skim
    milk
4 heaping tablespoons soy powder
1⅓ teaspoons granulated sugar substitute
½ teaspoon sea salt

Put milk, cottage cheese, eggs, honey, maple flavor,
and oil in blender and mix for 1 minute. Add powdered skim milk,
soy powder, sugar substitute, and sea salt and blend 1 minute.
Pour into saucepan and cook over very low flame till thickened,
stirring constantly. Pour into custard cups or small glasses and let
cool. Put in freezer and when semihard, insert a stick in center.
When frozen solid, immerse bottom half of glass or custard cup
in hot water till loosened.   *Makes 8 frozen-on-a-stick bars.*

Each bar has
16 grams of complete protein
197 calories

Frozen Yummy On-a-Stick

> 2 cups skim milk
> 4 eggs
> 1 teaspoon vanilla
> 4 tablespoons honey
> 2 tablespoons safflower oil
> 4 heaping tablespoons noninstant powdered skim
>   milk
> 4 heaping tablespoons soy powder
> 1⅓ teaspoons granulated sugar substitute
> ½ teaspoon sea salt

Put milk, eggs, vanilla, honey, and oil in blender for 30 seconds. Add powdered skim milk, soy powder, sugar substitute, and sea salt and blend another 30 seconds. Pour into saucepan and cook over very low flame till thickened, stirring constantly. Pour into custard cups and let cool. Put in freezer and when semihard, insert a stick in the center. When frozen, run hot water over bottom of dish until dessert is loosened.

Makes 8 frozen-on-a-stick bars.

Each bar has
12 grams of complete protein
186 calories

Spicy Apple Cream

> 4 eggs
> 1 cup skim milk
> 2 tablespoons safflower oil
> 2 apples, cut up
> 1⅓ teaspoons granulated sugar substitute

½ teaspoon sea salt
½ teaspoon cinnamon
¼ teaspoon nutmeg
½ cup noninstant powdered skim milk
½ cup soy powder
2 tablespoons lemon juice

Put eggs, skim milk, safflower oil, and apples in blender for 30 seconds. Add sugar substitute, sea salt, cinnamon, nutmeg, powdered skim milk, soy powder, and lemon juice and blend another 45 seconds. Pour into pan and cook very slowly over very low flame, stirring constantly, When it thickens, pour into dessert dishes. *Makes 4 servings.*

Each serving has
21 grams of complete protein
304 calories

Chart of Complete Protein

		Protein Grams	Calories
CHEESE			
American or Cheddar	1 cup, grated	36	497
	1 thin slice for sandwich	8	133
	3½ oz. solid	25	398
Bleu or Roquefort	½ cup	21	368
	1 tablespoon	2½	46
Cottage cheese	½ cup	20	120
made with skim milk	½ cup	24	75
Parmesan	1 cup, grated	48	524
Ricotta	1 pound	62	481
Swiss	½ cup, grated	27	370
	1 thin slice for sandwich	9	123
	3½ oz. solid	27	370

	Protein Grams	Calories
EGGS		
Whole egg 1	6	75
Egg yolk 1	3	59
Egg white 1	3	16
MILK		
Whole milk 1 quart	32	640
1 cup	8	160
Skim milk 1 quart	36	360
1 cup	9	90
Buttermilk 1 quart	36	352
1 cup	9	88
Powdered skim milk, noninstant 1 cup	54	540
1 heaping tablespoon	7	70
NUTS		
Almonds ⅔ cup	19	547
Pecans 1 cup	9	696
Walnuts, chopped 1 cup	21	628
SEEDS		
Pumpkin seeds ½ cup	29	553
Sesame seeds ½ cup	14	423
Sunflower seeds ½ cup	18	420
SOYBEANS		
Soybeans, uncooked ½ cup	34	403
cooked (they absorb a lot of water) 1 cup	22	260
Soy grits, uncooked ½ cup	34	403
cooked 1 cup	34	403
Soy powder, low fat 1 cup	43	356
1 heaping tablespoon	7	59

		Protein Grams	Calories
WHEAT GERM	1 cup	26	363
	1 tablespoon	3	49

YEAST

		Protein Grams	Calories
Powdered brewer's yeast	1 heaping tablespoon	10	55
YOGURT 1 cup		8	120

FOR COMPARISON

MEAT AND POULTRY, COOKED

	Protein Grams	Calories
Bacon, 3 fried strips	5	147
Beef meat pie, 1 individual pie	17	443
Chicken, broiler ¼ lb.	20	151
Chicken meat pie, 1 individual pie	16	503
Chili con carne (without beans), ⅔ cup	9	203
Club steak, ¼ lb.	24	260
Corned beef hash, ½ cup	10	229
Duck, roasted, ¼ lb.	23	310
Frankfurter	7	124
Hamburger, ¼ lb.	22	224
Ham, canned, ¼ lb.	16	142
Lamb, chop, ¼ lb.	15	102
Lamb, loin chop, ¼ lb.	13	103
Lamb, leg of, ¼ lb.	14	96
Liver, beef, ¼ lb.	20	136
Liver, calves, ¼ lb.	19	141
Rib roast of beef, ¼ lb.	14	151
Pork chop, ¼ lb.	16	260
Tenderloin steak, ¼ lb.	17	148
Turkey, roasted, ¼ lb.	27	265

Fish and Seafood

	Protein Grams	Calories
Clams, steamed 4 oz. (4 large or 9 small)	14	82
Codfish, broiled, 4 oz.	26	162
Crabmeat, cooked, 3 oz.	14	90
Flounder, 3½ oz.	17	79
Haddock, 3½ oz.	20	165
Halibut, 3½ oz.	21	100
Lobster, ½ average (3½ oz. of meat)	18	92
Oysters, raw, 8 med·	8	85
Salmon, canned, 3 oz.	17	120
Sardines, canned in oil, 3 oz.	24	203
Shrimp, steamed, 3 oz.	23	110
Sole, 3½ oz.	17	79
Scallops, 3½ oz.	23	112
Tuna, canned in oil, 3 oz.	24	288

Good Things to Know

HERE ARE some basics I learned when I first got into nutrition, and they may help you too. I wish there were a hipper way of getting into them, but a down-to-earth approach seems best.

Blackstrap Molasses A by-product of sugar refining. It's one of the richest sources of iron, inositol (a B vitamin), and calcium, and it tastes good.

Calcium If you want calm nerves, calcium is for you. Most of the calcium in the body is in the teeth and bones, but the rest is used by the nervous system. When buying calcium, get the pills that include magnesium. For calcium to be absorbed in the body, you must take some fat or oil with it (use whole milk instead of skim, or if you drink skim milk, have a salad with oil in the dressing). Vitamin D must also be present in the body for calcium to be absorbed and used.

Calorie A unit expressing the heat output of an organism and the fuel or energy value of food.

Carbohydrates   Sugars and starches.

Carob Powder   Also known as St. John's Bread. It's a dried plant substance with a taste very similar to chocolate, but better for you.

Cholesterol   A fat-like substance found in the blood and the brain. It is present in many foods and can be manufactured by the body. In natural foods containing fat there is always a combination of cholesterol and lecithin, which is a fat dissolver. Without lecithin, cholesterol can build up in the arteries, causing the blood supply to the heart to be diminished. Food processing eliminates lecithin, so you should take this separately.

Collagen   A cement-like material that holds all your cells together and helps keep your skin plump and juicy. Protein and vitamin C are needed to form collagen, and calcium stiffens it to a gelatine-like substance. If the collagen isn't strong (from a lack of protein, vitamin C, or calcium), harmful substances such as cold viruses or disease germs can penetrate it. Blood-vessel walls also consist of collagen, and bruises and bleeding gums result from a lack of strong collagen.

Gram   A metric unit of mass (weight) equal to 15.432 grains, one-one thousandth of a kilogram. 100 grams equal 3½ ounces.

Lactose   The most important sugar, found only in milk. Because it digests less rapidly than other sugars, it isn't fattening, so you can drink lots of milk.

Lecithin   Occurs in natural, unprocessed foods. It dissolves cholesterol, and when taken separately as a supplement, will dissolve any excess cholesterol in the body. Fantastic for your nervous system and skin, so take it daily with yeast.

Magnesium   A mineral important to the nervous system and found in green leaves. It is lost in discarded cooking water. When buying calcium pills look for a combination of calcium and magnesium.

Milligram   A unit of one-one thousandth of a gram, equal to 0.0154 grains.

Sea Salt   Salt from the sea, containing many valuable minerals.

Skim Milk   Noninstant powdered skim milk dissolves much easier than the instant. Instant powdered skim milk will make food gummy, gritty and stringy.

Sugar Substitute   Any form of artificial sweetener (without which life would be very dull—at least food would be). There are three forms: liquid, in which several drops equal one teaspoon of sugar; a tablet, which equals one teaspoon of sugar, but dissolves only in hot liquid; and granulated, similar in form to granulated sugar, but one-third teaspoon equals two teaspoons of sugar. The granulated form comes in individual packets, each containing one-third teaspoon, but it is more economical and easier to use in bulk, with each level teaspoon containing sweetener comparable to 6 teaspoons of sugar. There are no calories in most artificial sweeteners, although a few contain minor amounts. All the sweetened recipes in this book use the granulated form in bulk.

Vegetable Oil Natural vegetable oils (safflower, soybean, corn, sunflower, etc.) are the principal sources of linoleic acid, one of the three essential fatty acids needed to form adrenal and sex hormones and necessary for good skin and glossy hair.

Vitamins A group of food factors necessary for the normal function of cells and essential to maintain life.

Vitamin A Essential to good skin (prevents and clears up infections of the skin), shiny hair, day vision and particularly night vision, cell growth, and resisting infections. Vitamin A and vitamin E work together because without vitamin E, vitamin A is destroyed by oxygen. Vitamin A is found in green and yellow vegetables and apricots. The National Research Council recommends 5,000 units of vitamin A a day, but I take 50,000 units a day and believe that 25,000 units a day should be a minimum. Vitamins A and D are the only vitamins that can be toxic, but only in massive doses.

Vitamin B Complex The B vitamins are B1, B2, B6, B12, biotin, folic acid, inositol, niacin, pantothenic acid and PABA (para amino benzoic acid). All the B vitamins are water-soluble and can't be stored in the body, so they should be taken every day. They are synergistic, which means that one alone or several together increase the need for the rest of them. They are necessary for steady nerves, healthy eyes and skin, and the richest source of *all* the B vitamins is powdered yeast.

Vitamin C Ascorbic acid. Nobel Prize-winner Linus Pauling recommends 3,000 mg. a day, but I take 6,000 mg. a day and more if I feel a cold, virus, or sore throat coming on. I haven't been sick one day since I started this a few years ago. One glass of orange juice supplies 100 mg. The only way to get much more is with ascorbic acid tablets (much less expensive than the "natural" vitamin C tablets, and according to Linus Pauling there is no difference chemically). Vitamin C is water-soluble and can't be stored in the body, so the body tissues should be saturated with it every day. When a virus or foreign substance tries to invade the body, it attacks the vitamin C, destroys it, and is destroyed by it in the process (the reason for massive daily doses). It works best when calcium is present in the body, so be sure to drink lots of milk or take calcium/magnesium tablets every day. Smoking uses up 25 mg. per cigarette, so if you smoke or use aspirin, or sugar substitutes, or anti-histamine, or any drug remedy, or have any allergy, take plenty of vitamin C (ascorbic acid) to de-toxify them all.

Vitamin D   Known as the sunshine vitamin, vitamin D helps the body absorb calcium and retain it (without vitamin D much calcium is lost). Foods contain little, so it's wise to take either 50,000 units once a week, or 25,000 units twice a week. Vitamin D can't be absorbed without fat or oil, so take it after a meal that includes some oil, or after a tablespoon of vegetable oil in the morning. Vitamin D, like vitamin A, can be toxic, but only in massive doses.

Vitamin E   An oxygenizer, it helps all muscles in the body by lowering the demands of oxygen. With increased oxygen, the heart can do less pumping. Vitamin E is also known as the sex vitamin and helps produce normal sex hormones. Vitamin E adds additional oxygen to the brain and has been used to help mentally retarded children. Wheat germ, wheat-germ oil, and soybean oil are the richest sources of vitamin E. I take six 200-unit capsules a day, but people with any kind of heart condition should possibly take 1500 units a day. Works best with vitamin A, so be sure you take enough of that vitamin too.

Wheat Germ   The source of new growth in each kernel of wheat. It contains complete protein and is one of the richest sources of vitamin E. You should eat it untoasted, for strong heat destroys some of the vitamins.

Yogurt   A form of fermented milk or lactic acid, which is full of the B vitamins and helps digestion. Whenever I wake up in the middle of the night with things on my mind and can't get to sleep, I take 10 calcium-magnesium tablets with half a cup of yogurt, go back to bed, and in minutes I'm zonked. Yogurt is pre-digested milk, so it works *fast.*

Suggested Supplements

Yeast	2 tablespoons in morning in orange juice (see below)
(powdered)	2 tablespoons at night in milk (see below)
Lecithin	2 tablespoons in morning with yeast in orange juice
	2 tablespoons at night with yeast in milk
Safflower Oil	1 tablespoon in morning
	1 tablespoon in evening (in salad)
Vitamin A	25,000 units in morning
	25,000 units at night
Vitamin B	(Get plenty in yeast)
Vitamin C	4 500-milligram tablets in morning
(ascorbic acid)	4 500-milligram tablets at night
Vitamin D	1 50,000-unit capsule *once a week* (Sunday)
Vitamin E	2 200-unit capsules in morning
	2 200-unit capsules at night

187

Calcium and	
Magnesium	6 dolomite pills in morning (calcium 130 milligrams, magnesium 78 milligrams) 6 dolomite pills at night

Don't start out with the quantities of yeast given above. Work up to them gradually, following the instructions in Chapter 1.

Instead of mixing yeast and lecithin separately in the morning and again at night, you may want to put 4 tablespoons of each in a blender with either orange juice or milk or whatever liquid you like, and drink smaller quantities throughout the day.

I put 2 cups of skim milk and 1 tablespoon of safflower oil in my blender, turn it on, add 4 tablespoons of yeast, 4 tablespoons of lecithin, 1 teaspoon of sugar substitute, and 1 teaspoon of maple flavor, chill, and *voilá*—a maple malted. I drink half of this every morning, the rest in the evening, and I love it.

Everybody is different and has different requirements. You might feel that you need more Vitamin E, for example, and take 1200 units a day instead of the 800 units suggested above. Experiment until you find what makes you feel best. Only Vitamins A and D can be toxic and then only when taken in enormous quantities.

If you feel you need additional B vitamins, be sure you look at the label and see that there are equal amounts of Vitamins B1, B2, and B6. Most brands contain larger quantities of the cheaper Vitamin B1 and less of the more expensive B6, but it's important that they be equal. Several brands supply this.

Important Books

Let's Eat Right to Keep Fit by Adelle Davis

The basic and best book on nutrition. Easy and interesting to read.

Let's Get Well by Adelle Davis

This goes into more detail on specific problems and ills. After digesting her other book, try this one. You won't be disappointed.

Vitamin C and the Common Cold by Linus Pauling

A fascinating book by the brilliant Nobel Prize winner. You will learn that Vitamin C may not be a vitamin at all, but a function of the liver which man lost millions of years ago and which most animals still retain.

Vitamin E Your Key to a Healthy Heart (The Suppressed Record of the Curative Values of This Remarkable Vitamin) by Herbert Bailey

You'll learn how a barrier against Vitamin E has been built in this country by the medical traditionalists of the AMA at the same time that it's being used with spectacular results in such medically advanced countries as England, Germany, France, Italy, and Russia. It

shows scientific data proving remarkable cures using massive doses.
Stay Young Longer by Linda Clark
A terrific book on natural "Wonder Foods" and nutrition written with a light touch.
Psycho-Cybernetics by Maxwell Maltz, M.D.
If I were stranded on a desert island, this is one of five books I wouldn't want to be without. It's brilliantly written about "self-image psychology." I've read it maybe fifteen times and it's great!
10 Days to a Great New Life by William E. Edwards
One of the better "self-help" books. (If you've gotten yourself to take yeast, lecithin, and vites every day, this book is for you!)
Power Through Constructive Thinking by Emmett Fox
If you read only one section, "The Seven Day Mental Diet" (pages 188 to 198), this may change your whole life—but let me warn you it's tougher than any diet you've ever tried!

Index

Eggs:
  Argentine, 28
  Greek, 26
  in-a-Basket, 29
  Oriental, 28
  Parisiens, 25
  Roman, 35
  Russian, 30
  Scrambled, 24
  Scrambled Mardi Gras, 31
Egg Soup, 52

Farmer's Garden Salad, 79
Florentine Eggs, 26
Flourless Cake, 142
Fluff Puffs, 41
Fried Cheese 'n' Chili Balls, 38
Fritters:
  Apple, 13
  Honey Almond, 14
Frozen Maple Cream Bars, 175
Frozen Yummy Custard Bars, 176
Fruit Topping, 124

Greek Casserole, 59
Greek Eggs, 26
Green Beans, Armenian, 95

Hangover Heavenly, 15
Hardcooked Egg Salad Dressing, 129
Hollandaise Sauce, 117
Honey Almond Crunchers (cookies),
  150
Honey Almond Fritters, 14
Honey Dressing, 133
Hot Chili 'n' Bean Soup, 53
Hot Cole Slaw, 88
Hot Mustard Sauce, 118
Hubbard Squash, Stuffed, 105

Irish Rarebit, 63

Italian Cheese Cakes, 149
Italian Pancakes, 12
Italian Pudding, 166
Italian Risotto Soup, 58
Italian Stuffed Eggplant, 107

Lemon Soup, 50
Lemony Sauce, 114
Light and Dark Crunchers, 150

Macaroni, 69
Macaroons, 149
Maple Molasses Syrup, 112
Marinated Eggplant Cubes, 42
Mashed Turnips, 104
Mayonnaise:
  Marvy, 122
  Uncooked, 122
Mexican Chili Sauce, 124
Mexican Eggs, 27
Mexican Rarebit, 66
Minestrone Soup, 57
Mocha Cream, 169
Mocha Marvy (drink), 18
Molasses Fruit Cookies, 152
Molasses Nut Bread, 153
Molasses Puffins, 154
Molasses Zing (pudding), 170
Moscow Dressing, 130
Mozzarella Peppers, 38
Muffins:
  Raisin Bran, 151
  Whole Wheat, 8
Mushroom Pilaf, 64

No-Flour Cake, 142
Nut Nilsson (pudding), 173

Okra Soup, 58
Onion Sauce, 120
Onion Soufflé, 30